OUT OF THE ROUGH

OUT OF THE ROUGH

England in Zimbabwe and New Zealand

Peter Baxter, David Lloyd
and Jonathan Agnew

ANDRE DEUTSCH

First published in 1997 by
André Deutsch Limited
a subsidiary of VCI plc
106 Great Russell Street
London WC1B 3LJ

A CIP record for this title is available
from the British Library

ISBN 0 233 99158 1

Typeset by Derek Doyle & Associates
Mold, Flintshire.
Printed and bound by WBC, Bridgend.

Contents

PROLOGUE

Gatwick, 25 November 1996

DAVID LLOYD
'Assemble at the Copthorne Hotel, Gatwick Airport' is the instruction to the team and they're all here. The big coffin cricket cases with bright new labels are lined up. There are autographs to sign, interviews to give and some shocking haircuts to inspect. Everyone's looking spick and span.

I'm very excited, as we all are. I'm conscious that there is an overview that this winter's just preparation for the Australians. It's not. We're off tonight to Zimbabwe and I know Zimbabwe. The first objective is to win there. Then we have to move on to New Zealand and win there and come back with the nucleus of a team that'll take us forward in our domestic season.

We're full of anticipation, raring to go. There's a terrific feeling within the camp. After all the preparation and our fitness training in Portugal and all the theory of it, we're looking forward to getting to Zimbabwe and getting on with it and putting it into practice. I know that we're fit enough and I know that we'll need to be.

But, at the moment, number one, I'm looking forward to these new business class seats. I'm thinking, 'Those'll be nice. I'm looking forward to a little snooze there.'

PETER BAXTER
I'm just doing the Zimbabwe leg of the tour, which makes it quite a short one for me. Cricket tours don't get much briefer

1

than six weeks. But sitting in the departure lounge, even for a mere camp follower there is an inevitable thrill of apprehension about a journey to a new country – especially for the broadcaster who has got to make it work. My box of wires, microphones, sound mixer and suchlike has cleared its security check and is, I hope, being loaded into the hold of BA 53 as I sit in the departure lounge.

A posse of the hard core of the press group accompanying the tour begins to form. It is like the beginning of term. In most cases we haven't seen each other since the season ended in September, but we'll be living in each other's pockets for the next few weeks. I'm getting a lot of, 'No Aggers, then? He'll have his feet up by the fire, I suppose.'

'Yes,' I say. 'Let's ring him.'

JONATHAN AGNEW

The phone rings on a November evening and there's Backers, with a few other familiar voices in the background adding their own comments. It is a funny feeling to think of them all sitting at the airport, waiting for the call to the aircraft to start another tour. It becomes so much part of our lives as cricket journalists.

Peter Baxter has kindly undertaken the first part of the winter trip, which will give me a chance of Christmas at home with my family for a change. But this evening I've heard the usual interviews on the radio with the departing players and I wonder how I'll feel when the First Test starts thousands of miles away and I'm tuning in to 'Test Match Special'.

1

WELCOME TO HARARE

PETER BAXTER
It is just after nine o'clock in the morning in Zimbabwe and the British Airways jumbo looks out of place as it comes to rest in front of Harare Airport's low-key terminal building after its overnight flight from a wintry Gatwick to the heat of Southern Africa. And it is hot.

DAVID LLOYD
I've been here before. Last winter, in fact, with the Under-19s, so I know exactly what to expect. Chaos coming through immigration, but luckily we get ferried through. Then we see one little bus arranged to carry us and our massive pile of baggage. But I remain so calm I can hardly believe it – and it's just because I've been before. I've been in this hotel before, too. Last year we were the only people in it – sixteen of us – while it was being refurbished, so it was a soulless place and I still have nightmares about it. I can't wait to see the front entrance, because when we were here then there was a gang laying the paving stones at the front and I clocked it very early on that as fast as they layed them during the day there was someone coming along at night and pinching them. So I thought, if that has carried on they'll not have finished yet. But they have.

We've travelled a long way; we're a bit hot and sweaty in our nice dark suits. I think we look really smart and

3

businesslike and we are here for business. But we are ushered straight into what can only be described as a greenhouse for a briefing on the do's and don'ts of Harare, like the street-sellers and people wanting to exchange money and warnings about Aids, which obviously doesn't concern us, but there's plenty of it around here from what we are told. I wonder how much of the Zimbabwe Cricket Union officials we shall see again on the tour.

We're all looking forward to the tour ahead, especially our big fast bowler, Alan Mullally. He's asked how he's going to spend any time off. 'Aw, chill out on the beach and get some surfing.' It's going to come as a shock to him when he finds out that Zimbabwe's a land-locked country.

PB

For the England team there is an official welcome. For the accompanying journalists the officials are rather less welcoming. Immigration officers issue us with slips of paper which they say are temporary visas for the press, which must be officially ratified at the Ministry of Information within forty-eight hours. And then there is Customs. The photographers in our party are pounced on by officers convinced that they are on the point of selling their only means of earning a living – their cameras – on the black market. One of them reveals the huge bag of film he is carrying. 'How many films do you have there?' asks the customs officer.

'Oh, about a hundred.'

'Well, I want to see them all when you leave.'

'But I'm going to use them to take pictures.'

The customs officer has the last word. 'Then I want to see all your negatives.'

Happily, by some oversight, the more mysterious radio mixer, microphones, headphones and assorted wires I am carrying on behalf of 'Test Match Special' do not attract the same attention, but it is four hours and a trip into the city centre later before the photographers and their cameras are

4

allowed into the country.

As I drive from the airport the seven or eight miles into Harare, I am inevitably making comparisons with South Africa and our tour during the previous English winter. Things here are on a smaller scale at first sight. It appears less sophisticated (though South Africa in plenty of areas can come up with a notable lack of sophistication). Here you can be in no doubt that you are in Africa. The quip of the late Brian Redhead on Radio 4's 'Today' programme, in the early days after the city changed its name from Salisbury, is spinning in my head. 'Hip, hip Harare.' Soon I am to learn that the *Sun* newspaper takes it up to herald the restart of their correspondent John Etheridge's regular tour diary. Their headline reads, 'HIP HIP HARARE, HE'S BACK WITH HIS DIARY.' Oh dear.

There is still the Ministry of Information to be confronted – and discovered through an unmarked doorway off a shopping arcade. In fact, the issuing of a small green press card and the restamping of passports is accomplished with charm and reasonable haste. Now the tour can begin.

On the second evening both team and press are invited for a reception at the British High Commissioner's residence. This sort of occasion was a feature of my first few tours, but, probably with the massive increase in the size of the accompanying press party, has often on recent tours not included them. I suspect that it can only do so now because at this early stage we are not up to full strength.

The residence is magnificently sited and we gather on a terrace by a sweeping lawn and gardens which seem to go on for ever and hide any trace of an African capital city just down the hill. Some of the guests, delighted to see a full England team in Zimbabwe, are pressing them to visit schools and hospitals, but they have left themselves a short enough preparation and acclimatisation time and the answer has to be, 'We're here to work.' I just hope that this valuable public relations side of a tour, again a feature of so many tours in the past, is not completely ignored.

5

DL

We are practising, in these early days, at the Alexandra Club, which sounds nice but it's years behind the times. The head groundsman is called Davidson. He's got a lovely pair of wellies and a yellow boiler suit. I make the suggestion that he and his crew might step on it a bit to get the nets ready, because we're due to start at 9.30. But I'm told, 'They don't get here till eight and then they sit down for a cup of tea. Then they get their suits on.' I look at one lad's suit and there's more rip than cloth. They go at their own pace, but absolutely spot on 9.30 the last peg of the guys holding up the nets goes in.

We've been promised six net bowlers, but none materialises and when we ask about them we're told, 'No, there are none available', which is pretty normal. So we make do. We find James Kirtley from Sussex and Matthew Rawnsley from Worcester playing locally. Matthew is a slow left-armer and James is a quick bowler who did very well in the TCCB XI against South Africa 'A' last summer. I am amazed at the confidence of the pair of them. They're keen to impress and they do.

There are some early problems with the captain and Andrew Caddick both having arrived with a cold and the physiotherapist, Wayne Morton, catching it from them. That doesn't put Wayne off from tireless net bowling, despite having had an operation on each ankle just before he came out. He gets his reward as I am videoing the net practice when he bowls the captain and then has him caught at second slip. Atherton wants it erased from the tape, but Morton wants it saved for posterity – to show his grandchildren.

Jack Russell asks to be filmed keeping to the spinners and immediately takes the first one from young Rawnsley straight in the mouth. There are always these early little knocks, though I can't believe that two of the bowlers have come out with brand-new boots, so they're suffering with blisters.

The nets are a bit narrow and confining and so we concentrate a lot on practice on the open wicket in the middle of the ground. Pairs of batsmen have a good forty minutes together in the middle – ten overs or so. It's better to get people running round and simulating match conditions. We are at altitude, too. I may have missed a trick there with the Under-19s, because I didn't realise then that Harare is 5,000 feet up, so now I can see that they did brilliantly because a four-over spell for the quicker bowlers is enough at this stage.

I am standing as umpire in these practice games and I'm impressed by Phil Tufnell's commitment. What a character – but deadly serious when he bowls. He's thinking all the time and he's very critical of his own performance. He'll be the focus of attention and I accept that. He's been saying to the manager, 'I've got to see a lion or an elephant, Mr Barclay. I want to see a big cat.' John Emburey takes some of them out to have dinner with some people he knows at their house and Phil strokes a big cat. It's a huge cheetah that is in the hallway – stuffed. He's happy now. He doesn't need to see one that's running about.

I've been with Alec Stewart, Alan Mullally and Nick Knight to what we thought was a steak restaurant, but it's a game restaurant and they eat ostrich, zebra, wildebeest and kudu. (I'm asked, 'What's a kudu?' – 'Well, it either moos or neighs, or summat like that.') After that meal I'm watching them with interest to see how they get through the day, but they seem all right, they're not leaping over the stumps yet.

We hear a rumour that the Zimbabweans wanted to put Graeme Hick and Kevin Curran in the teams to play against us in the opening matches at the weekend. That gets my hair up a bit. 'Have you not enough players of your own?' In fact they've selected strong enough sides for those two one-day games, so they're obviously looking to win. In my mind, privately, without saying as much to our lads, after four or five nets, being on Zim. soil with Zim. umpires, right in the middle of their season when we haven't played since

September, I'll be interested to see how we go. But we'll be playing to win and the only concession that we'll make is that everybody in the party plays over the first two matches.

PB

On a first visit to the Harare Sports Club, where the Boxing Day Test Match will be played, I get the chance to interview the impressive president of the Zimbabwe Cricket Union, Peter Chingoka, who tells me of the excitement of playing Test cricket against England. He is also grateful to the Test and County Cricket Board for having smoothed the passage, by forfeiting a large part of the usual tour fee. 'It's a small gesture for them. A very big gesture to us,' he says. The financial attractions of a tour by England were evident. 'Because it's such an attractive side, commerce and industry is buzzing around and taking a very keen interest in it. That can only do the sport a lot of good.'

Down at the nets, the Zimbabwe team have been practising, so I am able to meet the captain, Alistair Campbell. He endorses the president's emphasis on the importance of this tour to his country's cricket future. 'We've never had such a big exposure to the world's media as we're going to have on this tour. So it's make or break time for a lot of guys. They can build their careers from just one or two innings in the series and if we can pull off a victory, that'll be even better for Zimbabwean cricket. And you know, from this series the Zimbabwe Cricket Union have got a lot of income and hopefully that can go into the development areas and some black guys can be coming through and we can be very competitive five years down the line.' Campbell does not give the impression of a man overawed to be facing a country with 115 years' greater experience of Test cricket than his own.

Acting on the time-honoured military dictum that time spent in reconnaissance is never wasted, I decide to drive the fifteen miles out of Harare to the Harare South Country Club the day before the opening match there against a Country Districts XI. It turns out to be a lovely little ground, ringed by rather spare trees and adjoining the club's golf course. In fact it is very reminiscent of some of the country grounds in Australia, with accompanying eucalyptus trees. A few temporary stands have been erected to give enough room for a Saturday crowd of perhaps 500. There are tents round the perimeter also. Is one of them the press tent, I wonder? Eventually I discover a pile of red telephones in a corner of the clubhouse verandah, conveniently situated at square leg. They are all apparently wired in but without either numbers or dialling tone. There are no telecom engineers to be found, nor any sort of an official from the club.

Eventually a man in shorts and sandals introduces himself as the president of the club and confirms that that verandah corner will indeed serve as the press box. I warn him that there may be a few more of us than he is anticipating. Surprisingly, without too much rancour, he comments, 'You know, my family has been farming here for seventy-five years and we've been trying to get a phone line all that time. You bastards come along and get them just like that. Maybe I should order mine through British Telecom.' He also reveals the final irony that he himself had to build the small exchange for this event. Mind you, the phones are still not working. I just hope they do tomorrow.

I have seen the occasional person around Harare carrying a mobile phone in the past few days. That would be a very useful back-up for communication to and from the BBC. In the town I see a shop advertising proudly that it supplies these adjuncts to modern living. There they are in a glass case inside the shop. 'Are these now operational in Zimbabwe?' I ask.

The reply starts, 'Well, actually . . .', and I know they are not.

There are mobile phone advertisements in the papers. I ring up to make enquiries. 'The man who knows about them is not here.' He is not here at any of the companies concerned. Then, reviewing the problem, I realise that, although I have seen mobile phones being carried and attached to people's belts, I have not yet seen any being used. We really do need those land lines to work tomorrow from Harare South.

2

OPENING SHOTS

PETER BAXTER
The clouds look ominous to the south of Harare as I leave the city again on the road that is romantically signposted to South Africa, even though the border is about 360 miles away. At least at 7.30 in the morning the traffic is a bit lighter than in the middle of yesterday.

It is sunny enough as I arrive at the Country Club, but the telephones are still not working and stay in that condition until two hours into the day's play, though the club manager provides his office phone for the Press Association and the BBC to get some sort of news out.

The photographers set up their processing and wire machines on the stage of the club's hall where, no doubt, if they cared to stay, they could take part in the children's pantomime in a month's time. An alarming-looking antelope's head is discovered in the wings, but they spread themselves out and prepare to do the show right here.

DAVID LLOYD
This is an out-ground, if you like. It's a game which is a bit of fun and the people have gone to a lot of trouble to get things right, but we are keen to get off to a good start.

We decide to have a bowl first, because it's nice to get the bowlers through their actions and into some sort of rhythm. Young Chris Silverwood is absolutely thrilled that he's got

11

his England shirt on. He's quite nervous. He feels just as he did making his debut for Yorkshire. He's gone from having the target of a place in the 'A' Team to leap-frogging into the senior side, so it's a great day for him but he's maybe a bit disappointed that he doesn't bowl a little bit better. But he does get a wicket and it's a Test player – John Rennie – caught behind to end a useful partnership.

The press are writing our opposition up as a bunch of farmers. If that was me they were writing about, I'd be a bit put out by it. It doesn't matter to us what line of business they're in. There may be a dentist playing, or an estate agent, but 'farmer' seems attractive. You might as well say that Jack Simmons is a draughtsman, which he is. Michael Watkinson, the Lancashire captain, is an engineer. These are all first-class cricketers.

PB

Indeed there are six Test players in the Country Districts ranks and, at this early stage, some of England's bowling looks a little rusty as they are seriously affected by the heat. So getting them down to 198 for 9 by the forty-sixth of their fifty overs is a fair achievement in the circumstances.

By now, though, there are spots of rain and, worryingly, great forks of lightning splitting the darkening skies. As the players head for the safety of the clubhouse, the heavens really open and the rain comes down vengefully. In the next hour, two and a quarter inches fall on the outfield – and not insignificant amounts on the occupants of the fringes of the press verandah – and the ground is reduced to a series of lakes an inch or two deep in places.

DL

I think some of those puddles are a foot deep. Little children are running round and diving in the pools and Phil Tufnell comes out and does a mime act of fly-fishing in one of the big ponds that have formed. At least it gives us the chance to do justice to the magnificent lunch. The ladies who lay them on take a lot of trouble. It would do Jack Simmons proud.

With all this water on the ground, I say to one of the umpires, 'Can we clear off?'

'No,' he says. 'We're looking to start a 25-over game in three-quarters of an hour.'

I ask, 'Where are we playing?'

'Oh no, this will clear.'

But of course it doesn't, and finally the umpires agree that the weather has beaten us and the game is off.

PB

Telephone contact with Britain, having triumphantly been established, now becomes intermittent and so, as the local farming community takes advantage of the excuse for a good session in the bar, the rest of us head back for Harare.

The following day, being Sunday, attracts a fair crowd to the Harare Sports Club, to see the Zimbabwe Cricket Union President's XI take on England in another one-day match.

I have done a recce of this ground during the week and even met some telecom engineers who, encouragingly, seemed to know about all our requirements. The commentary box, which will also be used for the Second Test Match, seems ideal in most respects. Except, at eight o'clock this morning, in communications. The telecom engineers who are to do all the connections and identify our broadcast wires do not appear until the game is starting at 9.30. So an eventful first hour is reported on for Radio Five Live by Pat Murphy from the press tent switchboard.

I hope we are getting our problems out of the way early. I hope the same applies to England, too. They are batting first and are soon reduced to 24 for 3 by a familiar name – Eddo Brandes – who bowled them out at Albury Wodonga in Australia in the 1992 World Cup.

DL

All our discussion before the game has been that this is a decent side we are up against and it's not an Arundel-style

13

run-out, but again we get that line for Brandes – 'the big chicken farmer'. He is a big lad, too, but he's played in the Lancashire League and he bowls admirably, with good line, length and pace, and swings the ball. He may be a one-spell bowler, though. We'll see. He does get a bit of clatter when he comes back.

PB

Alec Stewart is joined by Nasser Hussain in a restorative stand, which adds 133 over the next 33 overs. Stewart goes on to his hundred and Hussain gets fifty.

As England's fortunes improve, so do the BBC's. I have discovered some bared wires hidden behind the ZBC's commentary box door which are labelled 'BBC'. I still have to find a telecom engineer to make them long enough for us to use. (Commentary from behind a door offers limited possibilities.) This is our 'four-wire circuit', notorious sometimes for bringing crackly football commentaries from Eastern Europe. From us at the cricket ground it will travel to a sending station just outside Harare which will launch our voices into space and via a satellite to Britain and by land line again to Broadcasting House in London. It has humble beginnings, though, in this wooden commentary hut on stilts beside the sightscreen. Here I am twisting the four bare ends of wire on to leads which go into my sound mixer and then trying to experiment by trial and error to find out which wire is carrying my outgoing words and which will bring me a voice from London into my headphones. It is always an agonising period – and I have experienced it all over India, Pakistan and the West Indies – waiting for a reaction as one calls out, 'This is Harare calling London', while hearing only a hiss in the ears.

When at long last the answer comes, casually and apparently oblivious of the crisis of confidence at my end, 'Hello, Harare, this is London Control Room', it is an overwhelming relief. Now we can switch our reports to a proper microphone.

And the reports are of an England total which, while representing a recovery at 211 for 5, does not seem adequate. And so it proves. The President's XI win by five wickets with over four overs to spare. That is something of a drubbing.

DL

There are plus points. Alec Stewart has found good touch with his hundred and got good support from Nasser Hussain. So that is a pleasing part for us. But the rest of them find it a bit difficult having that first knock for quite some time. We had seven or eight weeks' off before we came here and we used that as a break. We also used it for fitness assessment, knowing that we were coming to altitude and heat and you need to be fit, so what you need beyond that is match practice and there's no substitute for being out in the middle, just getting a match situation into your system. But even with the limited preparation that we had we should have put a better show up than we have. That's life.

PB

Two days later comes the first first-class match of the tour, a four-day game against Mashonaland. To strengthen its base, the Zimbabwe Cricket Union has cut back its first-class teams to just two, Matabeleland being the other. In time they would like to see other regions of the country join in at this level.

Again there is a calamitous start for England, batting first. 7 for 3 and 78 for 5 when a thunderstorm halts play for two-and-a-half hours. The bowler who has accounted for captain Atherton and vice-captain Hussain is an Englishman, James Kirtley. When play resumes after the rain he gets two more – 4 for 44 in England's 175 for 9, so he is the centre of attention for the press.

DL

So in a funny sort of way it is a good day for England. James Kirtley from Sussex has pitched the ball up and swung it. He has bowled very well and I am delighted for him. He's been very much part of our preparation in the nets. He hasn't been told until six o'clock the previous evening that he's in the Mashonaland side, and when he is he's obviously decided to give it his best shot.

Robert Croft is playing well at the close and continues next morning supported by Phil Tufnell for an hour. We had that sign in our domestic season with 'the Cat' looking as if he's improving and enjoying his batting. He's disappointed to get out, but he gives James Kirtley a fifth wicket and Croft is left 80 not out.

PB

As Mashonaland start their reply to England's 197 David Lloyd and John Emburey have based themselves in the BBC box – happily in contact with the old country – to have a good look at the strengths and weaknesses of the opposition's Test batsmen from a better vantage point. They see David Houghton make 110.

DL

Dave Houghton plays beautifully. He's not afraid to go airborne, but he's a top-quality player. It does give us a nice insight into where they all play and that is noted, their strengths and weaknesses. Campbell, the captain, also makes runs and Grant Flower looks as if he likes to put on a bit of a show when he bats. Equally, they are assessing our bowlers.

The spinners are bowling in tandem and when they swap ends the ball suddenly starts to turn. By the end of the day they have four wickets each, and the next morning they are both keen to bowl and see who is going to get the first 'five for' of the tour. The Cat, Phil Tufnell, gets it in the third over and the lead has been kept to 83. The Zimbabwe players have looked to attack them to see what they are made of and they've come back strongly, sharing nine wickets.

A target of 250 might win us the match, but when we go

in we are embarrassed again, with the first three out for 22. John Crawley makes 74, but Mashonaland only need 98 to win and although Mullally gets two wickets at the start, they win by 7 wickets with a day to spare. The defeat just tells us that we need more match practice for the batting and bowling. The fielding has stood up well.

It's not my style to rant and rave in the dressing room. We analyse what has happened. It's important to give each other the signals that we know that we can play, because you can be sure there will be plenty of people writing about you that say you can't, and soon we get word back from England that we've got an absolute slagging off in the papers, which is a normal thing at home. Sometimes when you underperform you have to accept criticism, but it's a national pastime.

Among the articles faxed back I see that I have got a reputation for being 'gimmicky' for my use of videos of the players. That's just ignorance from the fellow who's written it, because it's just coaching. That's the way you do it and you do ask for total commitment. I can't understand why they don't see that. It's part of my job that I'm contracted to deal with the press. I don't go out of my way to ask for a press conference; I am asked to do it and I've got to answer questions they put to me.

Meanwhile a running joke – rather juvenile, I'm afraid – has started in the team with my assistant coach, John Emburey, known to us all as 'Ernie'. It started with, 'Do you want a cup of tea, Ern?' Then, when he is in his blazer, 'You look very natTEE, Ern', and later, 'There's no guarantee, Ern.' In the museum in Bulawayo, we shall have 'Is that a Grecian or a Roman, Ern?' Even Brian Johnston might have rejected some of those.

3

BULAWAYO

PETER BAXTER

As the team, having unsuccessfully asked for a one-day game to fill in the space left by the three-day defeat in Harare, head for a practice session at the Alexandra Sports Club again, I decide that it would be sensible to go to Bulawayo a day early. A potential problem has been raised a few days before when a casual conversation with Ian Robinson, the Zimbabwean Test Umpire, revealed that, contrary to the original itineraries released by the Test and County Cricket Board as late as September, the matches in Bulawayo are not all being played on the Queen's Club ground. That ground will still stage the first one-day international and the First Test, but the two games against Matabeleland will be played at the Bulawayo Athletic Club. I have asked the BBC in London to change the orders for the broadcast circuits and telephone to the BAC, but the shortness of the notice may be a problem. The first match is on Sunday and it is now Friday, so I set off early from Harare by road to drive the 300-odd miles to Zimbabwe's second city.

Once out of Harare, the road is clear and good, with the only hazard being overtaking slow-moving buses which belch noxious black exhaust fumes. There are occasional troupes of monkeys with admirable road-sense, an untended herd of goats with less of that quality and, spec-

18

tacularly soaring up as I drive past, a large bird of prey with a snake in its talons. The countryside unfolds in an African vista of grassland and trees and the four-and-a-half hours pass easily. Before I know it, I am into the wide streets of Bulawayo. (I have read that their width is to enable a span of oxen to be turned in the road, but I decide not to put that to the test.)

After checking into the hotel, I head immediately for the Bulawayo Athletic Club. There seems at first to be no one around as I walk through the clubhouse, but I can hear the sound of conversation from the bar, so I make for that. As I enter, all the chatter of the half-dozen people there stops and they look at me. There seems only one thing to say. 'Hello, I'm from the BBC.'

This provokes many immediate reactions. Most of them, I am relieved to hear, favourable. It seems that 'Auntie' is popular in these parts. The club chairman is at once welcoming and helpful, providing me with local telecom contacts and indicating the commentary box and press tent at the far end of the ground. The commentary box again has that happy sight, a wire carrying the legend 'BBC'. Telephones, however, appear more likely to be a problem. The order to move all the press phones from one ground to the other has reached Bulawayo rather too late. After a helpful discussion with the contact in the local telecom, I decide there is still a chance to have a preliminary recce at the Queen's Club.

It is only a little bigger than the BAC, with the clubhouse down one side, flanked by brick terraces topped with grass at each level. On the other side are trees and grass banks with the occasional log benches, though temporary scaffolding stands are also being erected for the visit of the English. There is a label outside a door announcing the club manager, so I introduce myself to the incumbent, who apologises that he has been in office less than a week – which does not sound like ideal timing – but identifies, from the plan he has been bequeathed, the commentary box. I am concerned that he might try to cram too many broadcasting stations into what is essentially a single commentary box. But we still have over a week to go and the army of television people has not yet arrived to rebuild the ground.

The next morning the team flies in from Harare, arriving too early for the hotel, who have no rooms ready, which means a long wait around the lobby. They won't be pleased, either, to see that the transport provided for their movement around Bulawayo is a small bus bearing on its sides the words 'BULAWAYO GIRLS' HIGH SCHOOL'. Photographers are quickly warned off. But in the afternoon the bus carries them to the BAC ground for some energetic, fast-moving fielding games.

DAVID LLOYD

In the past England's fielding practices have been accused of being dull, dreary and static. They're not now. They're active, short, sharp and competitive. In all of them involving cricket balls, they're not to mess up and I count the cock-ups. Dean Riddle, the fitness trainer, thinks these up and I have an input into it. People look at them and wonder what they're doing now, but we're working. This is our job. We run and it's explosive and you stop and you go sideways and you throw, catch or stop a cricket ball. I think it's dead simple.

The next day we have the one-day game against Matabeleland and it's good to see Nick Knight back to his true form, making 58. But we lose wickets at inconvenient times for one-day cricket. We never put big partnerships together, and when we do it takes too long. With no real acceleration to our innings, our total of 210 for 9 is a bit of a twitcher.

But the key is that Gough and Mullally bowl quickly and they bowl straight and a good length. Then Silverwood, who has had limited cricket but gives 150 per cent effort, with a nastiness about his bowling, suddenly 'hits his straps' and gets it in the right place with his action going properly. So that's three of them going well. Robert Croft gets a bit of stick in his first three overs. I see on the board that he's bowled three overs for 21 and I can't think where they have hit him, but he comes back to take three wickets for 42 and he's done his job and a little bit more. Suddenly we are starting to control the game, at 60 for 4 as late as the twenty-second over. We field brilliantly close to the wicket, with perhaps a bit to make up in the rest of the field.

John Emburey and I have been working with the team, telling them that we have total belief in them. 'Don't worry, don't fret. It'll come. We don't play Test Matches for another week. You'll be right.' And I think we will.

PB

England win convincingly enough in the end, by 59 runs. For all the confidence in the team itself, it is a relief to those of us who have to report the news to Britain. Again, the somewhat easy-going approach to the connection of tele-phones and broadcasting lines does give us anxious moments at the start and there are a few breaks in contact during the day. It is interesting to be told by one studio in London, after one of these breaks, 'I don't know if you realise, but we are having terrible problems at this end.'

And with victory comes a day off for team and journalists.

DL

On the Monday after that one-day win I have ordered everyone in the team to have a day off. They are not to touch a bat or a ball. So we can take advantage of the hospitality here. The Matabeleland and Zimbabwe and former Hampshire opening bowler Heath Streak's father, Dennis, who is manager of the Zimbabwe team, has invited us out to his magnificent farm, to relax, fish and shoot. When the two teams meet, of course, it'll be hammer and tongs, with no quarter asked or given, but this is a nice respect from both sides and the majority of us accept this hospitality. We are fishing for bream, but we catch gudgeon, which is a posh word for catfish. And we catch lots of them, but no great size.

21

This may well be the only day we do get off on this leg of the tour, so it's important to relax. It makes me surprised to read reports in quality papers that I'm hammering the work ethic, I'm austere, I don't let the lads out and they're living like monks. I am staggered, because I'm completely the opposite: 'Go and enjoy yourselves, lads. Relax in each other's company, have a good time, but tomorrow give me your best hour in the morning.' That's the way I am.

PB

After a further check on the progress of the Queen's Club, where I find that television also have designs on the one small commentary box, which necessitates further negotiations for another site for 'Test Match Special', I decide to go to the Matopos Hills. These weird rock kopjes include the bald rock known as World's View, chosen by Cecil Rhodes as the site for his grave. Sitting up there I find Jack Russell, painting the view that so enchanted Rhodes a hundred years ago. A hundred yards away down the curve of the rock sits Nick Knight, not so accomplished a painter and rather more coy about his efforts. Multi-coloured lizards dart out from the deep shadows of the huge boulders that surround the grave, to seize an insect and retreat as swiftly. There is a great feeling of peace and remoteness and a realisation of the enormous privilege of being able to see such places in the pursuit of cricket round the world.

Next day, 10 December, the four-day match against Matabeleland starts at the Bulawayo Athletic Club. England are put in, but a downpour halts play half an hour before lunch. By that time Henry Olonga, who won much attention in 1994 when he became the first black player to represent Zimbabwe in a Test Match, has attracted more by removing Mike Atherton's middle stump.

DL

The captain's form doesn't really worry me at this stage. It's always nice to get runs under the belt, but he's just been out of sorts within himself, so it would be a big ask if he got a big total at this time. People will say he's a big-match player, though.

But then it rains. And when it rains here, it rains. I think we're going to have to live with that all the time. It's rather like looking over 'Bill's mother's' at Old Trafford (the mythical place where all the bad weather comes from) – you know exactly when it's going to come. You can almost set your watch by it.

PB

Amazingly, after the deluge, when most of us are thinking of packing up and going back to the hotel, play restarts three-and-a-half hours later and, with the provision of an extra half hour (the timings throughout this match are the subject of some puzzlement and seem to depend mainly on the whim of the umpires, who cite local Matabeleland playing conditions), some progress is made. Nick Knight, after a chance at 38, reaches his hundred before the close, when England are 199 for 3.

We are sharing our commentary box not only with the Zimbabwe Broadcasting Corporation's local commentator, Trevor Williams, who doubles as the Matabeleland Cricket Association's treasurer, but also with the official scorers. This is obviously a useful arrangement for us, but it is also a pleasure, because the England scorer is Malcolm Ashton, who is an old friend. He scored for BBC Radio in the days when we covered county matches on Radio 2 and has done the odd day or two with us on 'Test Match Special', when Brian Johnston used to joke with him about his love of amateur dramatics. Now, in an English summer, he scores for BBC Television. His sense of fun and quick wit, not to mention his readiness to help with a statistic, make him good company during our five days in this box. We compare notes about some of the more amusing – and often gory – stories in the local paper, the *Bulawayo Chronicle*. One picture caption claims to show England's Kevin Ryan and Tony

23

Shuttleworth in action. That's funny, I haven't come across them on the tour. But they do bear a striking resemblance to Tufnell and Atherton. Could one of our party have been a little mischievous in briefing a local photographer?

We also enjoy the local weather forecasts. 'It will be dry unless it rains.' They are very rarely wrong about this.

When it rains, Malcolm borrows the home scorer's walkie-talkie to make contact with his fellow Lancastrian, David Lloyd. 'Can you confirm that we will be starting again in half an hour?'

'Yes.'

'And are we eating at Les Saisons restaurant tonight?'

'Roger.'

'Good. And don't call me Roger.'

'Roger and out.'

The next day England's batsmen add only another 135, though John Crawley makes 63, and are all out half an hour after lunch for 334.

DL

Nick Knight has played beautifully for his hundred, which is good for me and obviously good for him. That's another hundred. Hundreds in the bank just take a little bit of the pressure off. We have had a look at Olonga and Streak. They've had a good bowl, and in terms of Test Match cricket it's nice to see them.

Now our bowlers have had a bit of match practice and they're really, as they say, hitting their straps. We've rested Alan Mullally for this match but Darren Gough shows good pace and gives the first clue that, with them being big front-foot players, the short ball, fast and straight will pay dividends.

Gough has taken five for 62 by the close when we have them 181 for 9 and he's made them sit up a bit. I'm impressed with the wicket-keeper/batsman Wayne James, who makes 62, but he won't be in the Zimbabwe side, and I like the look of Mark Abrams. They have the experienced Mark Dekker in their side, who makes 26. He's a great lad. I might be doing him a disservice by calling him a farmer, but he looks like one and he talks like one. As soon as he's out he goes and has a beer, and when it's our turn to bat he comes over to us and says, 'I'm not looking forward to this. I hate fielding.'

PB

Dekker and his team mates have to field again, though, early the next day, after Matabeleland have avoided a follow-on that England were not thinking of enforcing. Gough gets the last wicket for figures of 6 for 64. They are all out for 188, 146 behind.

At last Atherton gets some runs, beginning to look more himself after a scratchy start until he is caught at mid-on off the slow left-arm bowler, Vaghmaria, for 55.

DL

That takes a bit of pressure off him and the rest of the team, because people focus on the captain and think that if he's not playing well the team isn't. He looked nothing like on top form. It's also important that Thorpe gets a half-century, because Graham, like Mike, has had indifferent form and I'm looking for him to get a big score. Stewart and Hussain get forties and we declare when Thorpe is out for 65, half an hour after tea on the third day.

Streak hasn't bowled in the innings, complaining of stiffness, and I'd have to say – and I hope this doesn't come back to haunt me – he just doesn't look fit. He looks heavy and laboured and a bit lumbering. If I was in their camp I would insist that he did bowl before the Test Match. That he doesn't bowl gives a signal to me that he's hiding something. But they are very keen for him to play in the Test.

PB

Matabeleland have been set 377 to win in the best part of four sessions of play. But the third day is abruptly ended by a ferocious thunderstorm, which has us frantically battening down the canvas curtains round our commentary box as the wind starts to lash the rain sideways. The operation causes the severing of one of our wires and, with forks of lightning jagging down all round us, I am a little apprehensive as I reach up to repair the damage.

The storm has left England effectively a day to bowl the opposition out.

DL

Dekker opens the batting and plays well. I think it's a feature of Zimbabwe cricket that they're never afraid to hit over the top. And while Dekker is scoring a very forceful hundred, after two early wickets for Gough, word comes through that Stuart Carlisle is going to open the batting for Zimbabwe in the Test Match, which is like a gift for us. Dekker is a far better player.

He puts on 156 for the third wicket with Heath Streak. He's a big, strapping lad and a strong, front-foot player who plays strong cricket. Our information is that he may not be such a good player of spin if you have an in-out field. That is, with catchers round the bat and deep fielders cutting off his big shots. His time at the crease, scoring 67, just adds to the mystery of why he didn't bowl, if they're keen for him to play.

Eventually he is bowled by Caddick, and Gough and Croft clean up the rest. We win by 115 runs with eleven overs to spare. Gough takes 5 for 75, so he's got eleven wickets in the match and he's never quiet, isn't that lad. He'll probably talk anybody through every delivery that he sent down. He's a smashing lad and it's good that he gets that reward. Croft has taken 4 for 65 and he continues to impress everybody. It's dead simple. He's got a rock-solid action. If he can put a sound Test Match temperament into that action he's going to be right.

Ronnie Irani has to come off the field in the middle of his third over with a bad back. Now, this is worrying, because it's the second time he's come off. The first time he came off with a groin strain, now he's got a back strain, which means that he's suffering somewhere, compensating and taking the pressure off various parts of his body.

Now we're into the business area of the tour and we feel we are prepared. We're prepared in fitness, prepared in heat and altitude, and now we've got some form with these two wins against Matabeleland.

The Saturday provides most of the players with their first sight of the Test ground, the Queen's Club, when we go for a practice there. We look round at all the preparations and say to ourselves, 'If this ground is ready for the One-Day International tomorrow, we'll be amazed.' But it will be.

PB

I have been paying daily visits to the Queen's Club during the week to see if there have been radical changes to our position. After the realisation that the original box I was shown would be full of television people, I was told that a platform would be built for us immediately underneath this box, raised about two feet off the ground. A subsequent visit revealed that a large scaffolding structure immediately beside this would effectively hide at least a third of the field of play from our sight. I have asked, therefore, if the platform supporting us could be brought forward almost to the boundary, to give us better lines of vision. It would also give us a better chance to see the face of the scoreboard, which is at an acute angle to our right.

On that Saturday afternoon, as England practise, I find that the low platform has been erected. It has been given an open-sided tent roof as well. Its only drawback is that the canvas screen erected down one side 'for our protection' has the effect of completely hiding the scoreboard from us. Memories of boy scouts with guy-ropes, though, give me the inspiration to sort out that problem quickly enough. However, the organisers do seem determined to make this a difficult place to commentate from. An enormous elephant's head is being erected on a scaffolding stand between us and the scoreboard. Closer inspection shows it to be a fibre-glass replica – an advertisement, apparently, for a taxidermist – but African elephants boast huge ears which would make better doors than windows. We now have to lean back in the commentary chairs to see behind the elephant's left ear and in front of the canvas screen. The elephant seems to pose a potential danger to players. Its tusks loom threateningly close to the boundary rope. One has the image of a fielder in hot pursuit of the ball ending up impaled on imitation ivory.

A telecom man is found to extend our wires to this gazebo of a commentary rostrum, which I gather will also have to accommodate the ZBC. We have a scheduled transmission to London to test the circuitry. That leads to a frustrating afternoon as I try to make contact, but eventually there they are, not so calm this time, as I am greeted with a testy, 'Where have you been?'

Still, it works. The 'Test Match Special' commentary team is starting to assemble, with the arrival of Henry Blofeld and Simon Mann in Bulawayo tonight, and tomorrow the international cricket will start.

DL

Our night before the big cricket features being made the victims of a Noel Edmonds 'Gotcha', when celebrities are 'set up' on his television show. I knew about it. So did John Barclay, the manager, but it's been so secret that when two fellows sidle up to him and say, 'Psst, we're from BBC Television', he's forgotten all about it.

The idea is that we've been set up to show some new revolutionary ideas for cricket equipment for a 'Tomorrow's World' feature. The players are given different things to demonstrate. There's a hat like a miner's helmet, with a lamp in it to help you to keep your head down over the ball when the spinners are bowling. Atherton wears that and Caddick tries a bat with a tapered shape and a spring-loaded handle. It's absolutely useless, but he has to go on and say how good it is. Jack Russell is sporting an enormous pair of wicket-keeping gloves. They are like dustbin lids. This has all been recorded before the four-day Matabeleland game.

On the last morning of that game I have told them that a pal of mine who used to manage a football club in England is sending along one of his trainers to give us some good luck tips. When this chap arrives he's a Zulu warrior who's come on to the ground and given them a warm-up in his full regalia, with his loin cloth and brandishing shield and spear. He's called George and he's got them all doing a war dance like a New Zealand 'haka'.

So on this Saturday night I manage to get them all into a room to watch a video. We've told them we can't use the team room, because the video's not working there. Jack Russell's the sharp one and he whispers to me, 'Where's the camera? I won't let on.' In fact the camera's hidden in some Christmas decorations round the TV set.

We sit down to watch this video with Dickie Bird sending us a message of encouragement. 'Good luck, lads. I know it's a big day for you tomorrow.' Then up behind his chair pops Noel Edmonds, because it's really live and we see those shots they've recorded. But it is all eventually turned on me.

Noel says, 'This is the bloke who's set you up.' I have visions of being thrown in the pool, but I just have sachets of sugar emptied over my head. Then Noel produces a numbers board, like the one in 'Question of Sport'. So I have to call out a number. 'Number four.' It's a picture of me doing some stupid dance.

'Do you recognise this man?'

'Yes, it's me.'

'Pick another number.'

'Seven.'

Another picture comes up and it's me, sitting at a bar in St Lucia with a mask and snorkel on. Because when that was taken it was Happy Hour and the crowd was about five-deep and you couldn't get to the bar. I was getting a bit irate and someone said, 'You've got to be noticed to get to the bar.' So I went back to my room and put the mask and snorkel on. I was noticed then. 'I'll have four lagers and three pina coladas.'

'Pick another number.'

The next piece is that never-to-be-forgotten 1974 Jeff Thomson to D. Lloyd – straight in the family jewels.

'What happened next?'

I just fall on the floor as if I'm in agony and I say, 'I can still feel that.'

We were just having some fun and it is a wonderful night for all of us. We are good and relaxed, all together. Team spirit, team effort. Next day it'll be business.

4

INTERNATIONAL EXCHANGES BEGIN

PETER BAXTER

After the team's commanding form against Matabeleland, it seems to both players and accompanying press that, as predicted by the management, the preparation period is complete and England are ready to play international cricket and to assert themselves against the youngest member of the international cricket family.

Bulawayo is beginning to fill up with visitors from Britain. Supporters' package tours are arriving and taking the restaurateurs of the town by surprise. In one or two establishments we have suggested to the proprietors that this might be a good week to break their normal custom and open on Sunday and Monday nights. They seem unaware of the potential extra business – a rush of it for Bulawayo – which is about to come their way. In the team hotel the night before the first one-day international the chaos is compounded by the other big event in town. ZANU PF, the government political party, have been having their party conference over the previous few days. The President, Robert Mugabe, has been here. The conference is ending today, but before going to the final session the delegates in this hotel have not checked out of their rooms and the new guests just arrived for the cricket are obliged to set up camp in the foyer, since the hotel staff are unwilling to throw powerful politicians, several of them government ministers, out of their rooms. That problem, which encompasses even Pat Arlott, the widow of John, is sorted out late in the evening.

Even Henry Blofeld, hot and bothered from the long journey from home, is a displaced person. Generously, I say, 'Come on, Blowers, I think you need some Bollinger.'

'My dear old thing,' says Blowers, doubtless amazed at such bounty from the BBC – and in Bulawayo, of all places. As a first-time visitor to Zimbabwe he has yet to discover the delights of Bohlinger beer. I hope that, even in his disappointment, he finds this cold liquid like champagne to a dry throat.

It is Sunday 15 December and I am at the ground by eight o'clock in the morning. I am a bit nervous about our communications from the Queen's Club as I set up our equipment under our tent at fine third man. I have scrounged some chairs and tables from various corners of the ground, connected all the wires, the phone is working, but there is no sound on the broadcast circuit. Conversations on the phone with the local telecom carrier make me think that the Sunday shift there is not quite as attuned to our requirements as the weekday staff. So the first few reports from Pat Murphy for Radio Five Live are by telephone before we make that welcome contact with Broadcasting House, though there are to be further technical hitches and extraordinary four-way conversations between myself, the Bulawayo and Harare carriers and British Telecom in London before everything is sorted out. But by then the game is well under way. Fortunately, our coverage is limited to quarter-hourly reports, at least until the closing stages.

DAVID LLOYD

The first question for us is Ronnie Irani. He's come off the field against Matabeleland saying, 'I'm stiff, I'm sore.' He's quite vital to the make-up of the side, particularly in a one-day team. I've talked to him and said, 'If you're 80 per cent, you can't play. You've got to be 100 per cent.' On this Sunday morning he doesn't have a reaction and says he's fit. So he plays, with the top six batsmen settled. Atherton will go in at number three, which seems to have caused some comment. The strategy is that Knight and Stewart should play in a very positive manner. If one gets out, Atherton comes in and the rest of the team play round Atherton.

As it is, after being put in to bat we get bowled out for 152 in 46 overs. We could not have played any worse. It looks a lovely pitch – a superb one-day batting strip. But it doesn't actually play like it. The ball stops, and there is this tennis ball bounce which works a bit against playing shots, and we don't even use the overs up. We get ourselves into an almighty jam and it looks as if they are eleven fellows who have just met.

We have problems with John Rennie. We've done our homework and asked, 'How does he bowl?' He bowls inswing deliveries on a strict off-stump and just outside line, but at nothing more than medium pace. And you think we can get after him, but it proves very difficult and the lads are coming into the dressing room and saying, he's a bit better than we thought he was. He's very difficult to score off. We're told that when he comes back in the closing overs he just bowls slow yorkers. At the end he's taken 3 for 27 in his eight overs, Streak has taken 3 for 30 and we're all out for 152.

In the dressing room we have to say, 'Right, that batting's finished. We'll talk about that some other time. You can't draw, you can only win or lose and to win you've got to bowl them out.' We have a determined dressing room, with upbeat chat, but they've got to go out and play.

Zimbabwe have usually opened, as far as I am aware, with the Flower brothers. This time they opt for Andy Waller, who's been around a long time. He's a 37-year-old who is a bush farmer, living out in the sticks. He opens the batting with Grant Flower and anchors the innings. We bowl well early on. The wickets we really want are the two Flowers and Houghton, and they score only 26 between them, but when Waller is run out by Hussain's throw to Gough for 48, the captain, Alistair Campbell, comes in at number seven. He would normally bat three or four. He's got a plaster on his face and it turns out that he's collided with someone in fielding practice. But it works out perfectly for them that they've got an experienced, established batsman when they're wobbling a bit at 106 for 7.

PB

Meanwhile all our problems are solved in the commentary tent and, as the finish looks like being rather closer than we might have expected after England's batting debacle, Garry Lineker's 'Sunday Sport' programme on Radio Five Live decides to favour us for commentary rather than the rival attraction of Bristol Rovers against Bristol City. It turns out for Pat Murphy and me to be a tense hour and a half's description of the end, particularly when Mullally has made an England victory almost probable with two wickets in two balls to reduce them to that 106 for 7. Croft gets Streak caught and bowled with the score at 137. The new batsman is Eddo Brandes. Campbell tells me afterwards that he just told the big man to play his own game.

DL

We set the field in for Brandes when he comes in, with us needing only two more wickets. We know he likes to hit it in the air, but this is his first ball. He just steps down the pitch and hits it over long-off for six. That's either brave or plain daft because, on that stopping pitch, he could have hit it straight up in the air and looked an absolute nana, but it went for six and that knocks the stuffing out of us. That single shot wins the game for them.

So Zimbabwe scrape through with eight wickets down. As a technical game it has been dreadful. As a spectacle, it's knife-edge. It's been disciplined bowling from us, but nevertheless we deserve to lose. There's a dressing room now where you could hear a pin drop. It's so quiet, as it should be, and you don't need to say a word. I don't think we batted too well.

We try to be upbeat, but you can't hide the disappointment, because you're just bracing yourself for a lot of criticism and on the batting front it's justified. But the batters will be the first to say, 'Sorry. Poor effort.'

PB

The usual scramble for post-match interviews is even more chaotic than usual. Satellite television take over the presentation of the Man-of-the-Match award in the players' stand, while the sponsors, British Airways, are setting up a rostrum for the purpose on the field of play. (Considering that the one-day series is being sponsored by a British company, it does seem to us – and particularly to the television people – surprising that none of us knew this either before we got here or even on the British Airways aeroplane that brought us. It smacks of not very effective media relations.)

Alistair Campbell, the Zimbabwe captain, is as helpful as ever, coming across to the press tent to talk to all of us, before having to accept his award all over again on the British Airways rostrum for the benefit of the cameras. Mike Atherton is besieged in the players' stand.

We have a system of compromise over these post-match interviews which has become established over the last few years. The BBC Radio man (in this case, myself) starts the press conference, sitting next to the captain, or whoever the victim might be, to do a straight interview, with the press taking notes. It avoids the player having to do it all over again with the same sort of questions and it does have the benefit of getting the press conference started with some sort of momentum. The down side is that we often feel we would get a better and more relaxed interview if we were doing it in more secluded circumstances. But then, so does each newspaper man.

35

DL

There are two clear days before the First Test. The first is a day off. I tell them, 'Go away. Clear off. Do what you want.' There are visits to the Matopos, a bit of golf or sight-seeing. Personally I just stay round the hotel pool and do a bit of reflecting and seethe a bit.

With his recent back problems this is seen as an opportunity to send Ronnie Irani for a scan. This proves easier said than done. We check on whether Bulawayo has the facility to do this and they haven't, so we have to get him to Harare. There's no convenient flight available, so we have to hire a car, and Wayne Morton takes him there after ensuring that they have the necessary equipment to do the job. They're back the same night in a four-seater aeroplane which gives them both a tale to tell when they get in. But now it's a question of whether Ronnie has any reaction, resting him and seeing how he makes it for the rest of the tour. Now we're aware that we might be a bit stretched for personnel, so wheels are put in motion for a replacement, depending on Ronnie's fitness, and at the end of the day we opt to contact Craig White, who's had an excellent time with the 'A' team in Australia. The question marks have always only been about his self-doubt, but on that tour he had to survive and he's come through with flying colours, having played very well with bat and ball in a team that gave a good account of themselves. The plan is that when he arrives in a week in Harare he won't just be covering Irani, but acting as a supplement to the squad. He'll be actively available for selection for both the Test and the one-day internationals. We want Irani to have the best possible chance to get himself right and fit and firing. We have also heard that Dominic Cork will definitely join us in New Zealand and he has assured us that he's raring to go. I wish he was here. He'd be flipping perfect out here.

PB

Now it's the eve of the First Test. England are chastened after Sunday's setback. While they prepare for the next day,

I have my preparations to make for the first-ever 'Test Match Special' from Zimbabwe. The players have been experiencing technical problems and I have not had a day's broadcasting on the tour yet without them, so I am apprehensive. First I have to deliver the passes for our two expert summarisers to their hotels. Both are staying very much on the outskirts of town. Trevor Bailey's accommodation turns out to be an English-style half-timbered pub which would not look out of place in a Surrey village, while Chris Cowdrey's place takes a bit more finding. It is a small lodge, which none of the locals seem to have heard of. Both are arriving in the evening, Trevor from Kariba and Chris from the Eastern Highlands area.

At the ground, the commentary rostrum has to be arranged for tomorrow. In the absence of any presence from the Zimbabwe Broadcasting Corporation, it falls to me to divide the area into three compartments with some hardboard screens that have been provided by the club. I put the ZBC position in between 'Test Match Special' and Radio Five Live, as they are only doing occasional bursts of commentary. Chairs and tables have to be found and commandeered. This is the glamour of outside broadcasting.

As I am running the two separate four-wire circuits to these two commentary desks, I am praying that tomorrow, for the first time on the tour, they will appear on time.

Ian Botham has appeared on time. There had been much publicity – as always when his name is involved – before we left England about David Lloyd's intention to involve him in team preparations. To many of these young players he was their boyhood hero and that is part of the inspirational purpose. (Though whether the great man is yet keen to sacrifice the 'one of the lads' status for the label of elder statesman may be open to doubt.) There he is now, in shorts and baseball cap – a huge presence, communicating his enthusiasm with a laugh never far from the surface. I have a wry smile, too, as I remember Botham the player, whose eagerness for net practice was not always entirely obvious, by his own admission.

5

AN HISTORIC INAUGURATION

PETER BAXTER

It is Wednesday 18 December. Another milestone in cricket history, the first time that Zimbabwe have met England, cricket's mother country, in a Test Match.

There is always a frisson for all those involved on the first morning of a Test Match, and particularly the first morning of a series. Not least for me with the nagging question, will it all work? I meet Andy Waller in the lift on the way to breakfast. A veteran of plenty of one-day internationals for Zimbabwe, today he will play his first Test at the age of 37. He has a nervous smile as we discuss whether he is anything near being the oldest Test debutant. (I check later that there have been thirteen who had passed forty before they played a Test.) Across the breakfast room I see Chris Silverwood and wonder if he might not also play his first Test today. He's sixteen years younger than Waller.

I think when it comes to laid-back Test venues, only the Sinhalese Sports Club in Colombo has come close to the casual atmosphere attending this match. With relief approaching incredulity, I find that both our broadcast lines are connected to London on time and we are in business. Even the gods of satellite communications must have a sense of occasion. The first worry is buried.

It soon becomes apparent that our open commentary tent is going to be something of a social centre – there is a constant flow of people passing in front of it as our team assembles. It is, for 'Test Match Special' on Radio Four long wave: Henry Blofeld, Simon Mann and myself, with Trevor Bailey and Chris Cowdrey to provide the expert comments and Jo King our excellent and supremely helpful scorer. Since start of play here is eight o'clock in the morning in Britain, we cannot start the commentary until after the 'Today' programme has finished on Radio Four at nine o'clock. But Pat Murphy will be providing the regular reports for Radio Five Live throughout the day.

DAVID LLOYD

For our team, we've decided on a twelve yesterday and this morning it comes down to a straight fight between Silverwood and Caddick. We go for Chris Silverwood. He's just coming into form and he bowled well in the one-day game. So it's a big day for him and he's absolutely thrilled to be winning his first Test cap. He's nervous as a kitten, of course.

It has been obvious to everyone for some time that our plan will be for Alec Stewart to keep wicket, and so Jack Russell, through no fault of his, will miss out in the interests of the balance of the side. He takes it so well and is fully supportive. He's a great team man. Ronnie Irani's back niggle has ruled him out of contention.

Alistair Campbell wins the toss and decides to bat. We get a wicket in the second over, caught at short leg off Gough. It seems inevitable that it's Stuart Carlisle. He's known as a walking wicket, which is very unkind, but it's the way it is. It's a perfect start, but then we bowl poorly in this first session. We have no control and at lunch they've reached 109 for 1, scoring at three-and-a-half an over on the first morning of a Test Match. Campbell is already 70 not out. So that needs to be put right.

To a certain extent we do put it right, with a couple of wickets in the afternoon session, and steady it down. It's Silverwood who breaks the second-wicket stand of 127 between Grant Flower and Campbell, when he has Flower caught at slip for 43. He takes a catch, too, getting under a skier at short third man to take Campbell off Croft for 84.

By the tea interval, though, they're developing another useful partnership between Houghton and Andy Flower and it's 200 for 3. But now the spinners start to take control. Croft gets Houghton caught after a bit of juggling behind the stumps by Alec Stewart. Then he has Andy Waller caught at short leg. Now we are back in it and by the end of the day we've taken the new ball and Silverwood's got a wicket with it – Guy Whittall, caught at gully. I think honours are quite even at the close of play with Zimbabwe on 256 for 6.

PB

Honours have been fairly even in the commentary tent, too. Blowers keeps telling me that it's the most enormous fun and he can't remember when he's enjoyed commentating on a day's Test cricket more. We have had only a minor technical hiccup when we could not hear the studio for a while, but I have found a loose wire, which explains that in the simplest way.

The producer for the satellite television company has been keen that their coverage is mentioned on the BBC in case they offer us any assistance. So I have mentioned that they have delayed the start of two sessions of play by having their presenter (to his own huge embarrassment) on the field of play as the first over is due to be bowled. I am not sure that that is the sort of credit they are looking for, but I do wonder aloud who is now running cricket.

DL

On the second day it begins to seem that early mornings are not our times. We only get one wicket before lunch when Paul Strang hits a full toss from Silverwood to mid-on, where Tufnell takes a diving catch. Strang has helped to add 79 for the seventh wicket with the wicket-keeper, Andy

Flower, who is 94 not out at lunch, by which time the 'knock 'em over in the first hour and let's get batting' plan has gone. We've still got some work to do.

It's better in the afternoon, when Flower has got his hundred. The end comes quite quickly with Tufnell getting Flower caught by a diving Alec Stewart, going for the sweep. He's not keen to go, but then he's not keen to go when you've knocked all three stumps out. Tufnell gets Olonga out, too, in the same over.

At the end of it they've got 376, after we've had two poor mornings, and 376 is only perhaps fifty over a decent effort by us. Around 320, bowling out a Test side on a hellishly flat pitch just after the first day, would have been all right, but 376 is maybe just in their favour. But we do know it's flat and that's important.

PB

Silverwood, with 3 for 63, has the best-looking figures, but Robert Croft's 3 for 77 is the product of 44 overs. This is the sort of news to delight the heart of one of our companions in the commentary tent, Edward Bevan. His main *raison d'être* on this tour is the presence of the Glamorgan off-spinner. Edward is doing regular reports for BBC Radio Wales and Radio Cymru in English and Welsh as well as putting together a television feature on Croft, so he has inevitably become the butt of a great deal of ribbing from his colleagues, not least from the former (briefly) Glamorgan player, Chris Cowdrey. Every time Croft does anything we call for Edward and suggest that all his reports start, 'Robert Croft comma'. He takes it all in very good part and even adds a few variations of his own.

DL

There is an hour to go before tea on the second day and it's a lively period, for Nick Knight particularly. The new ball gets knocked around and they're not bowling too well, either. Now the leg spinner, Paul Strang, comes into the attack and to the last ball before tea Athers plays back. He'll replay that one a million times. Get forward, kick it, do anything. But he's played back and paid the price. It just turned, straightened on him, and there's no argument with any decision, he's absolutely plum lbw.

PB

At this point, 48 for 1, with tea being taken, it starts to rain. It never gives us anything like the deluges we have witnessed in some parts already on this tour. This is steady drizzle, occasionally easing enough to raise hopes of a resumption. But under the TMS awning we are getting damp and beginning to establish where the leaks in the canvas are. If any of that water gets into our mixers we are in serious trouble, so there is hasty work with polythene bags. (This is sophisticated, near 21st-century broadcasting. . .) There are tricky decisions to be made about when it is safe to rejoin the mainstream of Radio 4, because there will not be a resumption of play during the timespan of the next programme. At the same time, interviewees have to be found, because Trevor Bailey and Chris Cowdrey appear to have exhausted all the angles of discussion on leg spinners. 'How about starting on left-arm seamers?' I suggest, in an effort to keep them going, while I haul someone across the ground from the clubhouse.

Our final guest at the microphone is the umpire, Ian Robinson, who is able to announce that they have just abandoned play for the day, although it does seem early to me, at 4.30, with an extra hour available. But Ian claims 'local knowledge' that the gloom will not lift, and he proves to be absolutely right.

DL

No problem with starting on time on the third morning. We lose Knight after three-quarters of an hour, hit on the ankle, full bung by Olonga. Out lbw for 56. Hussain comes in and is dropped at short leg first ball by poor Stuart Carlisle off

Paul Strang. Will it be an expensive miss? I think it may be. Carlisle's not having a great match.

Now we start to develop another partnership, between Stewart and Hussain. They've put on 68 by half an hour after lunch, when Stewart is lbw, hit on the front foot, sweeping the leg spinner. He's out for 48 and it's bitterly disappointing. Graham Thorpe comes and goes for 13. He's still slightly out of sorts and is caught at slip off Strang. But Hussain does look the part. He's playing it, as they say, with a piano stool. He's going really well.

There's been some talk about our batting order. We've got Stewart coming in at three. He's a regular number three for Surrey, while Atherton and Knight are regular openers. We didn't feel happy with what has sometimes been done in the past. If Stewart's been keeping wicket, Knight can move from six to one and vice versa. That's rather bitty. So we have talked to all the batters and said, 'If you all agree, that may look better and you'll all be more settled.' And they have all agreed. Now, it may be that Stewart is in one ball after a day keeping wicket, but he's prepared to live with that, because he thinks the top two are brilliant.

So that plan brings Crawley in now at number six, with a bit of a wobble on at 180 for 4. Crawley looks to mature and have presence and command at the crease with every innings that he plays. It begins to seem a long time ago that we had criticisms that he wasn't fit and that he needed to get his own house in order. Now he's done that to some tune, modified his technique, and when people say to me that we spend too much time on fitness, all I say is 'John Crawley'. What a terrific player he looks now. And he's become a good all-round fielder. He stands at short leg, fields in the deep, enjoys his fielding and enjoys the fitness aspect of his job. He's a very determined cricketer who's going to be a mainstay of our batting line-up for years to come.

Strang has taken three wickets now, but we reckon we're all right with him. He's a good leg spinner. He'd be excellent in county cricket. He's not the easiest to pick. He bowls a leg-spinner, a googly and something that comes out of the front of his hand, but it's not a flipper, it's just something that appears out of the front of his hand and it's a flatter, quicker ball that he's looking for you to play back to. When he played against Pakistan in October he had 5 for 80 at one stage and finished with 5 for 212. Wasim Akram got after him.

PB

At 180 for 4, with the last of the specialist batsmen together, England's position looks precarious at exactly the half-way point in the match – an hour before tea on the third day. But just before the end of the day Hussain reaches his third Test hundred of the year. At the close of play he and Crawley have added 126 together and it's 306 for 4. Seventy runs behind, there's plenty of talk about how England can now build up a big enough lead to force a win on the last day.

The 'Test Match Special' team, meanwhile, have witnessed a technological breakthrough of enormous proportions. Fred Trueman has sent us Christmas greetings by E-mail. Trevor is hugely impressed by this and we gather that Fred is so pleased with this new-found expertise in what seems to me to be a branch of the dark arts that he has also sent an E-mail to congratulate Yorkshire's new Test fast bowler, Chris Silverwood, and to trust that it will be the first cap of many.

There have been advances, too, in the case of the television on-field interview position. I must give them credit for having at last made the effort to be over the boundary before the umpires want play to begin. The only fly in the ointment has arisen when a left-arm bowler comes on at the city end of the ground and the sightscreen needs to be moved over. The equipment from that interview position has been stacked up against the sightscreen and a couple of technicians have to be brought to move it before the Test Match can continue.

The fourth morning starts as the third day finished, with

Crawley and Hussain batting on to close on the Zimbabwe total. The stand is broken by a remarkable catch on the fine leg boundary, when it seems certain that Hussain has just hooked Streak for six. Standing with his heels only just inside the boundary rope, Bryan Strang, a late inclusion in the side when Eddo Brandes turned his ankle, just holds up his left hand above his head and the ball sticks. There is a moment of disbelieving frozen silence as people can scarcely take in that he has caught it, not least the fielder and the batsman. Then Hussain turns for the pavilion, out for 113. Strang becomes, therefore, the first candidate for the 'Champagne Moment', which the 'Test Match Special' team choose at every Test to earn the winner a jereboam of Veuve Clicquot.

At 328 for 5, England are still 48 runs behind. By lunch they've also lost Croft, Gough and Silverwood and they're still nine runs behind.

When Mullally goes just after the interval, the lead is a precarious two runs and Crawley is just into the nineties, with the last man, Philip Tufnell, coming in to try to see him to his hundred. He couldn't have had a more staunch supporter. Strang certainly poses no threat to 'the Cat' and they manipulate the strike almost at will, eking out what runs they can while refusing many singles on offer as the Zimbabweans try for the chance to bowl at Tufnell. At last, with a rare burst of aggression in these circumstances, John Crawley goes to his century with a hook for six off Streak. It's another possible entry for the 'Champagne Moment'. Eventually it is Crawley who is out, caught behind for 112 to give Paul Strang his fifth wicket, and England have a lead of thirty. What a pity they could not have moved to that position a little more swiftly. The morning's batting has seemed to be rather cautious, as if there were more fear of an embarrassing defeat than a desire to seize the initiative.

DL

At the end there, Tufnell is playing the leg spinner as well as anyone and he has played him with soft hands and a good forward stride and he's never looked like getting out. When the last wicket falls, Tuffers is high and dry, two not out, looking for fifty. He fancies his batting now, though he does keep asking, 'How quick is he?' But he's proving a terrific tourist and his contribution here with the bat is a major one.

We've gone for a team of six batsmen and five bowlers, although Robert Croft can bat. I'd like to think that Darren Gough can bat. But they're blown away. Just knocked over. People say that it looks a long tail, but they've got to play around the batters or work out a system themselves.

We had been looking, with Crawley and Hussain in, for a substantial 500 and the chance to bowl them out. That was before that incredible catch by Bryan Strang. Normally the force of that would knock you over the boundary, but he has just stood there as if he were smoking a cigarette. I am pleased for him, because he's a grand lad and has great empathy with our dressing room.

Now we've got this lead of thirty and the important thing is that they've been frustrated – very frustrated. Things are not going right for them and there's been a bit of disagreement on the field between the captain, Campbell, the coach, Houghton, and the wicket-keeper, Andy Flower, who's another former captain. They come off the field flat, while we come off with a lead of thirty. 'Well played, Tuffers. Brilliant, John. You've scored a hundred. Let's go out and knock 'em over.'

We start their second innings with three-quarters of an hour to go before tea. Carlisle goes again, pushing Mullally into the off side this time, to be caught at silly point. Gough gets a perfect inswinger to Grant Flower. He's lbw and they're 6 for two.

The best players are coming now, Campbell, Houghton and Andy Flower. Croft is on for the sixteenth over. We've never really worked out how we're going to bowl at Campbell. We fancy getting him out caught at third or fourth slip, but he's not really hit it there. He and Houghton have crept it up to 27 for 2 at tea, just three runs behind.

They are 27 ahead when Croft gets one to rush on him. He's playing from the crease and he's bowled. That's a big bonus for us. Croft's such an influence now and a steady bowler. He's bowled this one flatter and fuller and deceived Campbell in flight and pace. That's a big wicket for us. And now Houghton has got to play an innings.

We've decided that they will be looking to play their strokes. We will try to cut off the big shots and still attack. Now Tufnell comes into the game. In his first over he has Andy Flower caught at short leg and then, just as we're getting towards the close of play, we get a really big wicket, David Houghton. We've got him just where we fancied him. We've cut him off in the big shots, so he's looking to play across the line. He tries to dink one into the on side and Croft takes the catch at short mid-wicket.

Houghton has got out at a really bad time, just before the close, and he looks annoyed with himself. It has left them 107 for 5 at the end of the fourth day. Effectively they're 77 for 5 and it's none of the lesser batsmen gone. It's the top five. We've a real sniff of victory now.

That's our talk. 'We're going to win this match. We're going to knock them over and then we're going to knock the runs off.' We're talking a great game, as you do. But they want to win as well. Sometimes you forget that. They're not just going to stand there and say, 'Bowl me out, I want to go back to the farm.'

PB

Fortunately on the final morning of the match, Sunday 22 December, we can start 'Test Match Special' only ten minutes into the day's play and take most of the morning session, though we will be missing about half an hour both before and after the lunch interval. Unfortunately, in the ten minutes while Radio 4 listeners are hearing the eight o'clock news, the first wicket has fallen. It is the night-watchman, Bryan Strang, who has slogged Tufnell back over his head in the third over of the morning for Mullally to take the catch. I cannot imagine that his captain will be delighted with him.

DL

We're right into them now, but Waller gets stuck in and he's been joined by Guy Whittall, who's handy coming in at eight. Now we don't have it our way. Waller hits a couple of big sixes and the runs are building up, and when those sixes go over it looks as though we're on the ropes a little bit. But half an hour before lunch he gets an absolute snorter from Gough, a fast, straight, rising ball that he gloves to slip. They're 178 for 7 – 148 ahead and plenty of the day still to go.

We take the new ball straight after lunch, but the spinners are on again after three overs. Croft gets Paul Strang caught bat-pad and then takes a great diving catch at cover to get rid of Whittall off Tufnell. I've been walking round the boundary, so I'm in just the right place to join in the 'TMS' teasing of Edward Bevan. 'I've never seen Goughie take a catch as good as that.' He's not fooled. He knows his man.

Chris Silverwood gets his first bowl for a long time, bowling at Henry Olonga – they're queuing up to bowl at Henry. He gets one to pitch on line and leave him. He nicks it. Thanks very much.

PB

Zimbabwe are all out for 234, a lead of 204. So the equation will be 205 to win with a minimum of 37 overs to go. Unless Paul Strang has bowled them into a potentially winning position, Zimbabwe are extremely unlikely to bowl any more overs than they have to, so the scoring rate required would be over five-and-a-half an over.

In the commentary tent we're asking, 'Will they go for them?' I am on with Chris Cowdrey. He was the sort of captain who would have had no hesitation in chasing this target, but he's not so sure that they will. 'We'll know when we see who's opening,' he says. 'If Stewart comes out with Knight, they're going for them. If it's Atherton, they're not.'

Then, perhaps losing faith in this theory, he asks me what I think.

I feel that Mike Atherton is often misunderstood and I think I am sure of his character. 'I think Atherton will open. And I think they will go for them,' is my version. All our eyes are on the low clubhouse on the western side of the ground to see who will emerge.

DL

You want to get the mood of the team when they come in off the field after bowling Zimbabwe out. There's no question. 'Right, we're going for these. We can get these.' There is no hesitation about it. This is where the captain takes over. I have very little to say. He's so positive. 'This is how we do it. Take every single. Get them on the back foot.' It's like a Sunday League match, but without the fielding circles or so much restriction on wides.

I am doing a little interview on television during the first couple of overs as Knight runs down the wicket to Streak's fourth ball and flat-bats him, tennis-style, for four through mid-wicket. The interview question changes. 'I was going to ask you if you were going for them. I don't think I need to now.'

We have to keep wickets in hand. Athers looks pumped up. His feet are moving again, the bat's going through, he's got quick hands and quick feet. But then he drags a ball on to his stumps from Olonga. He has been on song, but he's got nothing, really, and they've got their early breakthrough.

We've spent a lot of time talking about playing in partnerships. 'You're not playing for yourself. There's one team out there, that's you and him. So you play in pairs.' Knight and Stewart are together now, a great one-day combination. They get to work.

Zimbabwe decide to defend. They are not looking to take any wickets and I'm looking round and saying, 'Where are they going to get us out?' The way they have set the field, there are ones here and there. If you get a bad ball you'll knock it away and you'll always be ticking over at four an over. You might get a good over and get seven, so you'll always be round about that five-and-a-half as long as you don't lose wickets. We've decided to play till tea and see how we're going.

At tea, after five overs we're 36 for 1 with Knight and Stewart there. We're going at sevens. What a start. Most importantly, the Zimbabweans have come off visibly shocked that we're going for them. In our dressing room, our vice-captain, Nasser Hussain, says, 'If we score seventy in the next seventeen overs – and that's only four an over – with the field as it's set and these two still in, we'll have nine wickets in the last fifteen overs to score ninety.' Our team think there's only one winner. The other side cannot win.

After tea Stewart and Knight carry on with this breath-taking partnership. The opposition have got a real panic on. You can tell. David Houghton's the coach and Alistair Campbell's the captain, but suddenly you can see there's a strong Houghton influence out there. They start bowling wide down the leg side, interspersed with bouncers you can't reach. The match referee, Hanumant Singh, in his pre-match talk has spoken incessantly about 'the spirit of the game'. I wouldn't mind another word with him now. But we've got to get on with it.

The last fifteen overs have started with the second-wicket pair still there. It's 118 for one and we need another 87. This great Zimbabwean fielding side are having to work hard. There are fumbles here and there. Then Stewart skies a sweep off Paul Strang. He and Knight have put on 137 in 26 overs. It's 154 for 2 in the eighth of the last fifteen overs. It's a difficult time to come in and Hussain goes in the same over, caught at cover.

Now they're trying to keep Knight off strike and Strang's bowling to him over the wicket a metre down the leg side to the left-hander and spinning away, with two men behind. 'Good luck, Nick.'

John Crawley's in and he plays probably the best shot of

the game, going down the pitch to Whittall and smearing it to deep cover point, where Stuart Carlisle takes a great catch. At least he's got something from the game, after all. It's 178 for 4 in the twelfth over, and in the next over Thorpe is caught at slip off Streak. So at this stage we're steadily losing wickets, with only Knight going along his merry way.

We're now five wickets down and we need 21 off the last two overs. Gough's in now and he and Knight scramble eight off the fourteenth. Thirteen are needed off the last over to win the Test Match, and Knight's facing Streak. He nicks a two off the second ball. Off the third he plays a pick-up, swing, drag, pull, call it what you will, over square leg for six.

Heath Streak must have changed his underwear, because his next ball is fired wide down the off side, but it's a dot ball. So now we need five off two balls. The fifth ball is a scrambled two and now we want three to win from the last ball. There are nine fielders on the boundary edge. When I see that I think, that's it, you're spent. Whatever happens, the moral victory is ours. Knight gets a bat on that last ball and they run two, the ball is returned and they're run out by a furlong, though it takes a long time to get the ruling that it's Knight who's the one out for 96. The game is drawn, with the scores level.

PB

It is the first time it has happened in a Test Match. It is not a tie, because the batting side was not all out. The match was unfinished. It has provided us with a great afternoon's commentary on 'Test Match Special'. Henry Blofeld has been immovable for the last hour, thoroughly enjoying himself and telling anyone not quick enough to spot it for themselves, 'Gosh, this is exciting' – frequently.

We have all been shocked that some of the wider deliveries were not called wide, and Heath Streak later admits in a chat with the press that he himself has been surprised to get away with it to that extent. (My thoughts have returned to last year's Test at Port Elizabeth, were Dominic Cork was no-balled for a leg-side ball after a warning from umpire Cyril Mitchley for similar negative tactics.) Streak will later find himself fined by the match referee for his frankness – though, rightly appalled by that decision, the writers who have used his quotes will pay the fine for him.

Throughout the closing overs, David Lloyd has been pacing up and down anxiously on the boundary just beside our commentary tent. He is a man who gets very tense on behalf of his team. He is fiercely loyal to them and at the end is quickly across to the dressing room to see them. He may need to find the right words. They must be very disappointed to have fallen that whisker short of victory.

DL

One more ball would have done it. My emotions are running really high. All I say to our lads is, 'You've hammered them, you've absolutely hammered them. We get all the plusses from this game.' If Zimbabwe are elated at having saved that game, it's false elation, because they've had a right drubbing. And I can't wait for the next one.

6

THE AFTERMATH

PETER BAXTER

After an emotional finish like that there is a huge buzz round the Queen's clubhouse. The dressing rooms are at one end, with a small swimming pool behind and a dining room which is used at the close of play for press conferences. There are rumours around of harsh words having been spoken, fuelled by the adrenaline of a tight finish.

After he has talked to the press, David Lloyd comes and sits with me on a bench by the swimming pool to give his thoughts on the day. (It still seems a bit strange to be interviewing 'Bumble', our old colleague from the 'Test Match Special' box, in this capacity as England coach.) He uses many of the same phrases he has just used for the writers.

I ask him how his nerves are. 'Jangling, to say the least. I suppose that anyone listening to that game would say, "Terrific game of cricket". It'll go down in the annals of cricket as one of the best. The hard facts from our point of view – we've murdered 'em. Absolutely hammered 'em. When you get eight or nine fielders on the boundary and the ball flying down the leg side and over the batter's head, they're just clutching at straws. We won that. . . They were on the ropes. You're talking about people throwing the ball wide down the leg side. If that's the tactic and it's within the laws of the game, that's not for me to comment on. All

54

I would say is that I was here and I know that we've murdered 'em.'

DAVID LLOYD

I am going to get a lot of criticism for those words, but I would see it as just a northern turn of phrase. Where I come from, if Manchester United win one-nil we say, 'We murdered 'em, hammered 'em.' I've done possibly twenty interviews at the end of an historic drawn Test Match – that's no excuse. Emotions are running high, but I think that I am fairly calm. I don't think that I'm not in control. But my word, doesn't it cause a stir.

People in Zimbabwe latch on to it and, I sense, are quite offended by it, but that is not the intention, and I am sorry if I have offended anyone. Maybe I would be better off saying, 'England were in a position of some strength when the game ended.'

PB

So much material – reports and interviews – has to be sent down the line to London that we are de-rigging the equipment and wires in the dark and I am congratulating myself on having spotted that there would be no lighting in the tent and therefore taking the precaution of buying a torch when we arrived in Bulawayo.

Blowers is still on an adrenaline 'high' after describing the closing overs, while Simon Mann can be pleased with a successful first Test Match commentary. He has covered Tests before for Radio Five Live, but 'TMS' is a little different and, encouragingly, he has got better and better with increased confidence.

At the hotel we are sharing with both teams there is a great party in full swing in the bar. Members of the Barmy Army are there, treating one and all to their chant:

> When they ask us
> Who we are

Where we come from
Then we tell them
We are the English
The mighty, mighty English
We're Ath-er-ton's Barmy Army.

And on it goes.

David Lloyd is at the heart of it, called on to sing 'Sonny Boy' and 'Mammy' in as passable an imitation of Al Jolson as a lad from Accrington can do. Robert Croft leads Darren Gough and the congregation into an interesting variation of the French song 'Alouette', and when Alistair Campbell appears the Barmy Army greet him and his team-mates with a song.

You bowl wides, you know you do,
You bowl wides, you know you do.

And, to his credit, Campbell is joining in and signalling wide with the best of them.

DL
It's one of the joys of Test Cricket that both sides are together at the hotel having a sing-song a few hours after the end of the match. It's all good-natured banter. Robert Croft is the star of the show in true Tom Jones fashion. And after the Barmy Army, Bryan Strang comes back with a nice little bit of defiance, singing an African song, which is good.

The next day we have to get up to Harare, but it's the one chance to visit Victoria Falls, so we've hired two nine-seater aeroplanes. But only one turns up. The other pilot's got malaria. A bad cold would have done, but malaria it is. Eventually we manage to get fourteen on to the one plane and four get left behind. I'm one of them, with John Barclay, Mike Atherton and Chris Silverwood. We've then got to hire a car, and we drive to Harare in a Peugeot with a cracked windscreen, though it does, surprisingly, have air-conditioning. What we need is a pub lunch on the way, though the Midlands Hotel in Gweru is not quite like the Dog and Duck.

I hear later that on their rather cramped little aircraft to the Falls, Phil Tufnell has been stretched out in the aisle, fast asleep, while Malcolm Ashton, our scorer, and Dean Riddle, the fitness expert, have been so impressed that, on arrival, they have taken the immediate precaution of booking themselves on to a scheduled flight back to Harare in the evening.

Also arrived in Harare this evening is Craig White from a few days' break in Australia – our reinforcement, and it's good to see him.

PB

After seventeen days in Bulawayo, I think I am ready to move on, as I, too, take the road to Harare. We have all tested the culinary delights of Bulawayo to their fullest extent. The man whose sandwich shop has produced lunches to order for the commentary and press tents has already bid us a sad farewell. He reckons he has done enough trade in the fortnight to go on holiday now. He even broke the habit of a business lifetime and opened over the weekend, just for us – a fine entrepreneur.

My dining highlight has been at the Bulawayo Club, in company with Henry Blofeld and Mark Nicholas. It was like stepping back sixty years to the pre-war colonial days. Through a columned portico we went, up a sweeping staircase, round a colonnaded courtyard and into a dining room which would not have disgraced any of the great London clubs. Here I have not spied any portraits of Zimbabwe's president, though two or three of the Queen and the Duke of Edinburgh, looking very youthful, are prominently displayed. It has been an evening to savour.

Now, though, to Harare and Christmas.

7

CHRISTMAS

PETER BAXTER

It is Christmas Eve and the Second Test starts here in Harare on Boxing Day. (It is one of three, incidentally, starting that day round the world, in addition to England's under-19 team playing their 'Test' in Lahore. Christmas has become a busy time for international cricket.) So it is time for another recce to the Harare Sports Club. Fortunately, little has changed since the match against Mashonaland, nearly three weeks ago, though the spot I had earmarked for our Radio Five Live reporting position is now occupied by an air-conditioning unit for the television commentary box. I seek the ground manager, who is a very helpful Englishman, which is useful because he does understand the difference between Radios Four and Five. Generally in most overseas parts the BBC is the BBC, and to almost everyone that means the World Service. I have two alternatives for Pat Murphy's post. Either we erect a partition in the commentary box to section off a third of it, which will leave us with little space but will be convenient for power, broadcast lines and the telephone for emergencies, or we put a table and chair on the end of the television camera gantry beside our box, which will necessitate my persuading the telecom men to extend the wires, and our having to lay in an extra stock of batteries to power the equipment as well as having to erect some sort of shelter against the elements of fierce sun and equally fierce rain. The manager says that he is short of materials for a partition, so it may have to be the latter alternative.

I am going to enjoy some Christmas cheer now, though. A cousin of mine, whom I have not seen in thirty years, lives on a farm about fifty miles away amongst the strange rocks of that part of the countryside and I am off there for a family Christmas Eve dinner with all the trimmings; my first family Christmas for three years.

DAVID LLOYD

Christmas Eve nets have to be cancelled, because they've not covered that area and it's been saturated by a thunderstorm.

Christmas Day itself is very quiet. The Zimbabwe team mostly live round here and they're off with their families. Our families are not here. That's the decision we've taken – and this is our busiest period. The scheduled morning practice has to be cancelled again because of wet conditions, so we have an hour's session in the afternoon, which serves a purpose, though inevitably it rains again to curtail that. You've just got to get on with it, and that's been the key of this leg of the tour. The rains will come and the facilities are not terrific. 'Just get on with it, boys.'

Harare is like any city. You feel envious people saying, 'What a wonderful place Zimbabwe is – the game parks, Lake Kariba, Victoria Falls.' Fine. We play cricket. We see the hotel, we see the ground and we play, and when you get that day off, you've got to make it so special.

The tradition on Christmas Day in the team is that the new tourists have to put some sort of a show on. I am regarded as a new tourist, even though I had a Christmas on tour twenty-two years ago. I'm here in a new role, you see. So is John Emburey. (John Barclay is, too, I realise later. He was only assistant manager on the last tour and now he is tour manager, but he cleverly keeps a low profile.) The others are Robert Croft, Ronnie Irani, Nick Knight, Alan

Mullally and Chris Silverwood. Dean Riddle has taken the easy way out, flying home on Christmas Eve to arrive there today, ready for duty on the Rugby League bench tomorrow. Last year the team did a take-off of the Channel 4 racing, with each member of the team described as if he were a racehorse. This year we've done it in the style of the TV programme *Blockbusters*.

I've done the questions, featuring the twenty members of the tour. 'Which "C" is the Les Dawson of the guitar world?' That's John Crawley, because he's trying to learn the guitar. He's doing all right, but he hits a bum note every now and again.

'Which "S" guided his county to an epic one-day win in the most prestigious one-day competition in world cricket?' That's Alec Stewart, winning the Axa Equity and Law Sunday League with Surrey, which they are very proud of because it'll probably send them forward to win more things as the season develops.

'Which "C", as an Anglo/Welsh off-spinner, is known on his own patch as "Mr Blobby"'? Robert Croft, of course.

It's all just a bit of fun, so there's one against myself, obviously. 'Which "L" is rumoured to be in practice for a light heavyweight contest at Caesar's Palace?'

PB

I drive back to Harare on Christmas morning through my third police road-block in as many days. The purpose of these is so far a mystery to me. The day before yesterday I was just asked about the weather I had come through. Yesterday I was invited to 'poop the hooter', and today, it seemed, the reason for the barricade across the road was to wish me 'Happy Christmas'. I can't object to that, though there are many tales of road-blocks doing the rounds. At one the other day, I have been told, a gentleman so inebriated that he had to be helped from his car was asked to open his boot. He staggered round to the rear of the car where the policeman had to help him locate the keyhole. The boot was duly inspected and passed muster. The driver then had to be given further police assistance to regain his seat behind the wheel and, as he was trying to discover where he had left first gear in order to proceed on his merry way, the policeman bent down to the open window and said, 'You're lucky. Today we are checking boots, not drunk drivers.'

Back at the Harare Sports Club, I check on the state of things at the Test ground and find that the Radio Five Live partition has indeed been built in the commentary box. It is not a thing of beauty, being assembled out of bits of scrap timber, but it is a problem solved and that, to me, is as good as a Christmas present.

A less welcome present is to read the paper today. (Yes, the papers here publish on Christmas Day and New Year's Day, but not on Boxing Day or 2 January, which is, I suppose, quite logical for the staff who have to put them together.) In the letters section there are two reacting to the remarks made by David Lloyd immediately after the Bulawayo Test. One, from a judge, said that it was 'distasteful that the English coach should have made the loutish and unsporting remarks that he did about England having "murdered" Zimbabwe.' The other writer, commenting on a television appearance, said that he thought he must have been watching 'the commander of the Barmy Army which attaches itself to touring English teams, but I was shocked to find out that it was in fact the coach of the English team. It is sad to see that English cricket has sunk to such a level that it can appoint as its coach a man capable of making comments which seemed to me to be obviously inappropriate, undiplomatic and unsportsmanlike.'

Are they talking, I wonder, about my old friend Bumble? He seems to have put a few backs up. But that last correspondent does continue: 'Fortunately the balance was restored by the reasoned and sensible comments made by Mike Atherton the English captain.'

I do hope this is not setting the tone for an acrimonious tour, but I have a nasty feeling that the 'we murdered them'

61

quote will return to haunt David as Tony Greig's 'grovel' remarks did in 1976. Several of the newspapermen are having to write pieces reacting to these letters and allegations of other remarks made at the end of the Test. It is not something to increase the feel of Christmas spirit.

It is my sixth touring Christmas. My first, in 1981, was the rest day of the Delhi Test. The last one we had in Australia, too, was the rest day of a Test. Relationships between players and press have not always been cordial, although in most cases, on every tour I have been on, individuals have always been very friendly with each other, with only a few exceptions. The tradition on almost all these tours and, I believe, for many tours before I ever went on one, has been for the press to give a drinks party on Christmas morning. The large number of the players' families last year in South Africa made that impractical, particularly as many of the players had children with them. But this year the invitation to the party has as usual been issued, with a topical pantomime – a comparatively recent phenomenon, which a small press committee has been working on – thrown in. The invitation has been declined.

DL
At one of our team meetings in Bulawayo, after the manager has dealt with the usual administration – such matters as when you've got to get your bags packed by and so on – we have moved on to the entertainment department. That's Wayne Morton's pigeon. He's announced that we've been invited to the pantomime that the press are putting on. And there's an immediate crescendo of noise: 'You must be. . . joking. That's the last place we're going.'

We've been getting the newspaper cuttings faxed to us and I can't believe it. They're very negative. It's not everybody, but you tend to colour them all the same, which is disappointing. That same night that the decision was taken I'd had dinner with three of the pressmen organising the party, and of course it came up and they were very upset and I just said to them, 'They've had enough, they really have.'

In my own optimistic way I just hope it may be something that may be built on. But there's a lot of sarcasm and a lot of criticism that's just non-factual and completely wrong. It's nothing like what's happening. People say, 'Oh, well, they've got a job to do', but people are reading that and taking it as fact.

PB

I am dismayed by the team decision not to come to the press party. Our relationships with the players do not strike me as having been too bad. True, there is a style of journalism which depends on a clever, slightly cynical, turn of phrase and therefore probably also depends on things going wrong for England for its entertaining style. However, I remember the last touring Christmas pantomime, in Australia two years ago, in which the theme was captain and coach – Mike Atherton and Keith Fletcher – wandering in the wilderness in search of the solution and hearing the voice of God, or rather Raymond Illingworth. All parts were played by members of the press with every identifiable idiosyncrasy thrown in – to the huge amusement of all three targets and the rest of the team.

In India ten years ago I played a part in the creation of some song parodies, one of which recalled a fine first Test hundred by Tim Robinson – 'Ole Man Robbo'.

> He's not like Gower,
> He's not like Gatting,
> For some strange reason
> He keeps on batting.

Neither of those two took the little dig in any other than the humour of the occasion, though perhaps in fairness I should add that that was easily the happiest tour I have been on for press/player relations.

This rejection of the invitation will, I fear, cast a cloud over the tour which it scarcely needs. I am reminded of a remark from a member of the touring party early on, when I made some comment about paranoia in the team about the press. There was an instant and adamant reaction. 'Paranoia? Paranoia? That means it isn't true. This isn't paranoia.'

From conversations with one or two of the players I find that there is some embarrassment among individuals in the team. Usually it is only a few isolated articles that really cause the unhappiness, together with some of the more imaginative tabloid headlines. The brighter members of the team do realise that the reporters here do not write the headlines that accompany their pieces. They may also realise that the best way to deflect perceived poisoned pens is to start winning. When things are not going well for a team on the field, editors at home are always looking for their men in the field to reveal the true cause that they feel must lurk beneath the surface. Simply to say 'The opposition played better' is no answer. That is when stories of too many late nights – or not enough late nights – start to hatch.

It may be that an England team would prefer our press to be, like some others round the world, apologists for the team, writing only in blind support. I have sometimes detected in my colleagues a feeling that things going badly does make a better story (though I am not sure that applies to radio, where there is a tendency at home to shoot the messenger). I can see that this might become an irritant, but equally I am sure that the sycophancy I have seen in some other countries' press corps on tour would not appeal to most intelligent cricketers.

Though the inevitably lower-key press Christmas lunch lasts most of the afternoon, after those who have to do some work have done it, somehow it does not reach the joviality of some of its predecessors, even when the correspondent of the *Mail on Sunday* reads out a piece which might well fall into the 'sycophantic' category, written by the correspondent of a rival organ, the *News of the World*. The two of them joined forces to do a 'This is Your Life' on the correspondent of the *Daily Mirror*.

Back in a hotel room with just a few Christmas cards to remind me of the date, a call to my wife and children makes me wonder about the frame of mind of players similarly isolated from home on this day of all days and on the eve of an important battle.

8

THE SECOND TEST

PETER BAXTER
I have earmarked this as a potential disaster day for communications. It seems to have all the hallmarks in prospect. It has been three weeks since we broadcast from this ground – and then it was not always with instant success. It is a bank holiday, following the biggest holiday of the year. So I am amazed that when I plug in all the equipment, there is the identifying voice from the Broadcasting House Control Room in London.

There has been quite a lot of rain overnight, but play starts on time. England have brought in Craig White – only three days after he has arrived as a supplement to the team with the doubt over Irani – to replace Chris Silverwood, in an attempt to improve the balance of the side. Zimbabwe have made two changes. Eddo Brandes is fit again and replaces Bryan Strang, while the unfortunate Stuart Carlisle is left out in favour of the left-hander, Mark Dekker. In the commentary box Geoffrey Boycott has replaced Chris Cowdrey, who has returned home for Christmas, in 'Test Match Special's' only team change.

Alistair Campbell wins the toss and invites England to bat. We hear that England would have done the same had Atherton won. But in the first half-hour it looks as if it was a good toss to have lost.

DAVID LLOYD

The pitch is taking a thumbprint and so it will be slow. Will it stop a little bit, is the question. But, after the first exchanges, it looks all right. It looks easy-paced and it isn't doing too much, but I simply can't describe how slow the outfield is, so you don't get value for shots.

The problem is the grass. It's so lush and deep and they can't crop it to get it down to a length where the ball will travel quickly across it, and with last night's rain making it even more holding, the ball isn't going anywhere. The danger shot that we must pay attention to is the drive.

PB

But it is the flick down the leg side, the dreaded 'strangle', that brings the first wicket after a productive first half an hour, as Knight is caught behind off Olonga for 15. It is 24 for 1 and now scoring begins to look harder work. Stewart is missed at slip off Streak, but in the next over Atherton drives at Whittall and is caught at first slip for 13. In the over after that Streak gets his revenge, having Stewart caught at gully for 19. The morning now does not look quite so rosy for England, at 50 for 3.

It is 63 for 3 at lunch. Two extras come off the first two overs after the interval and then Streak strikes again, as Thorpe clips him off his toes straight to Dekker at short square leg to be out for 5, and half an hour later Streak persuades Hussain to edge a drive to the 'keeper and he is out for 11. It is 73 for 5 and England are in disarray.

John Crawley now needs someone to stay with him and White does so for an hour, before Whittall, whose slow-medium pace has been all but impossible to score off, has White caught low at slip by Campbell for 9. Croft helps Crawley add 34 in an hour either side of tea, but Whittall has him, too, caught at gully for 14.

At 128 for 7 there are still some unwanted records to avoid. The lowest Test score made in Zimbabwe is 139 and the lowest score made against Zimbabwe is 147. Both records are still vulnerable when Gough has a wholly inappropriate swipe at Paul Strang and is bowled for 2, and when the ninth wicket falls with Mullally caught and bowled by Whittall for nought. Somehow Tufnell looks altogether more dependable as he and Crawley limp through to the close of play at 137 for 9.

DL

We've lost six wickets to drives. The lads know that we've not done well. I can't explain Guy Whittall's figures at the end of the day. He's bowled thirteen overs, five maidens and taken 4 for 12. But I think their coach can explain it. He's the lucky bowler that they use. He comes on, breaks a partnership, and off. Today they couldn't get him off, because we kept driving. He's taken four wickets on a pitch that hasn't spat or turned square. He's not hit anybody on the gloves. We just got out. We played so poorly. John Crawley is 37 not out, by far the highest score, and he's played the tempo innings, just taking what's on offer, nothing extravagant. He's played Test Match tempo and a Test Match innings on that pitch. He's always had the temperament for it, I'm sure of that, and he's got the brains and he susses a situation.

Next morning the 'Cat', Phil Tufnell, hangs around to get us up to 156 and take fifty minutes out of the game. He's the last out, when he plays the new ball from Streak on to his stumps. He's only made nine, but he's helped Crawley get to 47 not out. Streak has finished with 4 for 43.

It's not a great score, but we get an early wicket when we come on to bowl. The new man, Mark Dekker, who scored that good hundred against us for Matabeleland, nicks an away-swinger from Alan Mullally to Stewart and they're 5 for 1.

PB

Twenty minutes after lunch it is 46 for 2, when White has Campbell caught at slip for 22, but it is the only other wicket England capture on this second day, because four balls after the tea interval rain calls a halt to what is threatening to become a very productive partnership between David Houghton and Grant Flower. They have already put on 47 for the third wicket, and it is 93 for 2.

The rain quickly makes it apparent to us that it does not intend to allow any further cricket this evening, with a violent deluge which has us battening down the large wooden shutters round our first-floor commentary hut as we finish off the day's broadcasting and get ourselves soaked in the dash for the car.

The rain lashes down on Harare for most of the night, and in the morning we discover that the covering of the square has not been adequate. There is a large marshy area on the edge, where a gully fielder would stand. There is no play before lunch.

DL

When we do get going after lunch on the third day, I've told the bowlers to be patient. The ball's not going to travel. The Zimbabweans will see it exactly as we've seen it, so bowl the line and bowl the length that makes it hard to score and they, by nature, will look to get on with it, as they do. They're not fussed about hitting it over the top and they're not fussed about playing across the line. Get it in the right areas and it will pay dividends. And we now do get it in those right areas. We get some good pace bowling from Darren Gough and some good holding again by Tufnell and Croft. They continue to look good in tandem.

PB

The Zimbabwean hundred comes up with still only two wickets down, though. Ten more runs are added by Grant Flower and David Houghton and now Zimbabwe are only 46 behind with eight wickets in hand. But then Gough gets the breakthrough, as Houghton is caught down the leg side for 29.

The Flower brothers add another 20 together before

umpire Russell Tiffin astonishes everyone – except perhaps the enthusiastic Gough – by upholding an appeal for lbw to dismiss Andy Flower for 6. So far, neither Tiffin nor his Sri Lankan colleague, K.T. Francis, have shown any inclination to accede to any such enquiries, entreaties or even demands by the bowlers of either side, and so this leg-stump yorker provides a bolt from the blue. Andy Waller quickly suffers the same fate at the hands of Tufnell as he presumes on the umpire's good nature by padding up. The next over Gough bowls Whittall off his pad and the chances of a big lead for Zimbabwe have diminished dramatically. It is 138 for 6.

If the giving or non-giving of lbw's has been quirky, we now have a strange umpiring decision. Throughout the tour, whenever Gough has given the signal that his slower ball is coming up, the slips and wicket-keeper have moved quickly in with the bowler. Now, suddenly, umpire Francis decides that this is sharp practice and jumps in to call 'dead ball'. In a flash of *déjà vu* I am transported back nine years to Faisalabad and umpire Shakoor Rana's objection to Mike Gatting moving a fielder late. Fortunately, despite some lengthy discussion with the umpires in the middle, this incident does not produce ramifications on quite the same scale and the word from the dressing room later is that after this match the practice will continue.

Gough's afternoon's work has forced England back into the match and at tea Zimbabwe are still behind, albeit by only one run. So much seems to have rested on the stoical shoulders of Grant Flower, who has been the rock of resistance while batsmen have come and gone at the other end. Immediately after tea, a drive over mid-off from him takes his side into a first innings lead, but he does not last much longer. Gough brings one in to him and Crawley dives forward at short mid-wicket to take the catch. Flower is out for 73 and Zimbabwe's lead is only three, with seven wickets down. Surely England can now end things quickly.

This is the moment, though, when run-scoring suddenly seems to become easier than at any other time in the game.

Paul Strang plays shots with freedom and finds support from the very capable Heath Streak, and 38 runs come in the next three-quarters of an hour. Croft ends the dangerous partnership when Streak gets an inside-edge on to his pad and Crawley is waiting at short leg to snap up the chance.

The large figure of Eddo Brandes appears with aggressive intent. When he has made one, he is caught on the mid-wicket boundary off Tufnell to the huge excitement of those England players and supporters who had not heard the call of 'no ball'. He then launches into Croft to hit him for a huge six over long on. Croft must have a little smile to himself as, next ball, Brandes tries to repeat the shot and is caught at long on. Croft adds the wicket of Olonga a couple of overs later. Zimbabwe have been bowled out for 215, losing their last eight wickets in three hours for 105 runs. Darren Gough, with his 4 for 40, looks at last to be back to the form that made him such a hero in Australia two years ago, and Croft has taken 3 for 39.

DL

So our 156 all out and out of the game has become very much back in the game when we're only 59 behind on first innings. Now we have to play better in the second innings and we do. We play with much more discipline, with more determination, and with more knowledge.

Athers is out of sorts, though, and we lose him on this third evening, playing firm-footed in the crease, caught at slip off Heath Streak in the third over. A quarter of an hour later the umpires decide that it is too dark to carry on. We are 17 for 1.

PB

As we are holding the fort up in the commentary box for 'Test Match Special', waiting for a convenient point to rejoin Radio Four programmes, we are joined by Gough and Croft. Darren Gough gives us an insight into the captain's state of mind after he has made 13 and 1 in the Test Match. 'Mike's always the same, whether he gets runs or not. He's a great player and I'm sure he'll come back in New Zealand and score lots of runs.'

Robert Croft expresses the view from the dressing room that they can get a lead of 300 and put Zimbabwe under pressure on the last day. At that Geoff Boycott cannot wait to get hold of the microphone. 'How many days do you think there are left in this Test Match?' he exclaims. 'Both teams have been scoring at about fifty runs a session. You're 42 behind now. Three sessions tomorrow; that's 150 runs. You're only going to be about a hundred on. Who's going to whack 'em? You and Goughie?'

Croft nobly sticks to the party line. 'I think they're going to be all out looking for the win, so there'll be a lot of attacking fields and so there'll be more gaps. So we might be able to pick it up with the outfield getting quicker.'

'And pigs might fly,' retorts the great Geoffrey. Despite this, they part with a good chuckle.

There is more rain in the night, but this time the groundsman gets his covering right and so play starts on time. We have had a bit of a scare on the 'Test Match Special' front when it has become apparent that our scheduled starting time is not until nearly half-way through the day. Feeling that this morning has the potential of being too critical to risk that, we secure a change of heart from the top of Radio Four and manage to broadcast commentary on a good slice of the morning's play.

DL

This fourth morning I am sitting with Ian Botham and plotting important matters. Where are we going to be fishing during the coming English summer and where are we going to be playing golf between the one-day internationals? So I'm a bit surprised when somebody drops in our laps a fax from England of a two-page article in today's *News of the World* under the headline 'MAKE ME THE BOSS. Ian Botham Exclusive. Lloyd bust-up.' Apparently Botham's not happy about this and he's not happy about that. He wants the job and he wants £150,000 to do it. So I immediately say to him, 'You don't want to take a cut from what I'm on.'

It's a hoot and we both howl with laughter, but it's in the *News of the World*, so the last I see of Beefy he's hot-footing it into the press tent, looking for their correspondent, David Norrie, who's lying low at this time.

The way Ian Botham has worked with the team is that we've said that he will have an informal involvement and work primarily with the bowlers. I don't want him just to work with the bowlers. I think he's got a role to play around everybody, but he has work to do for television as well, he's writing a column, he likes a game of golf, he wants to go off fishing. It's not all work for him, he's got to play. But when he's available, I can't stress it enough, if he's got an input and he wanders into the dressing room and he comes to the nets, that's fine, because the players are comfortable with him around. All the wickets, all the runs, all his experience are bound to rub off on some. So we could do without being told we've had a bust-up. It's just absolute nonsense.

A couple of days later I have a dinner date with the bloke who's written it, David Norrie. Do I say, 'No, I'm not coming'? No, of course I don't. I go with the other David Lloyd, from the London *Evening Standard*, and Peter Hayter. We've done it before on tour once or twice. Norrie's a bit sheepish; it's mentioned a little bit, but we brush it over. It's gone. You can't do anything about it. But David Lloyd's turned up with a bandage round his head. Apparently John Etheridge of the *Sun* has been having trouble sending his piece from his computer back to London and finally, in exasperation, he has stood up, shaken his computer, John Cleese-style. Then he has got his composure back and sat down to try again. Still it won't work, so he stands up and kicks the nearest chair, a plastic moulded one. The leg shears off and flies like a missile through the press tent and hits David Lloyd straight on the head. So he's got ten stitches under this bandage and he

73

does look like John Cleese in *Fawlty Towers* when the moose lands on his head.

Now it's my turn, as I'm doing my regular little piece for the *Daily Telegraph* about various things, adding that they want to watch it in the press tent or they'll be fined 25 per cent of their tour fee by the match referee. But we have had a good dinner and you can't beat them. You can't beat the press, because I end up paying for it. I've had to take Norrie out, because he paid last time.

PB

On this Sunday morning of the match, therefore, my first contact with the office has brought the unexpected observation from them: 'We're leading on this Botham story.' For some reason it seems always hard to get our offices at home to grasp the fact that the British papers – even worthy ones like the *News of the World* – do not appear under our doors every morning in southern Africa. So I have to ask for the story to be read out to me. I express the unpopular view that it does not sound like a major news item to me, but the name of Botham casts its own spell over sub-editors.

As the day's play gets under way, the presence of heavily armed guards gives us the tip-off that the President of Zimbabwe, Robert Mugabe, who is also the patron of the Zimbabwe Cricket Union, has come to the Test Match from his presidential palace, which is behind the high wall opposite the main entrance of the Harare Sports Club. His admiration of cricket and its values has been recorded in the past and I wonder, just wonder, if he would be prepared to give us an interview.

I find Don Arnott, the ZCU's chief executive, in the stable block-like offices of the Union behind our box and put my request. 'Let's see,' he says, more receptively than I had expected. We edge past the large men with bulging jackets on the approach to the VIP box. Eventually comes the answer. 'The President will meet TV, Radio and all the press a quarter of an hour before the lunch interval, and

74

then he is leaving.'

'Backers, I'd love to do that interview,' says Henry Blofeld. And so it is that Blowers meets Comrade Mugabe. 'What should I call him?' he asks as we make our way up the stairs, having left Simon Mann to hold the commentary.

'My dear old Excellency?' I hazard. Then, 'I think "Sir" will do, Blowers.'

It is a bit of a scrum in the box where he meets us all affably. 'May we have a few words for the BBC?' I ask and thrust Henry forward.

'Sir, you must be extremely pleased with the way Zimbabwe are coming through in this series so far,' he starts.

'Yes,' says the President, 'I am very happy that they have played so well against a side that has that tremendous experience and history of cricket.'

'And of course this tour will have done a great deal for Zimbabwean cricket.'

'Yes, and also I hope it has exposed a lot of the cricketers who haven't been here, and the admirers who have come from Britain, to our situation here and the fact that we are developing along proper lines in regard to sport across the field and we would want to see both whites and blacks play good sport and also get into the spirit of national unity, the spirit of one-ness in our country.'

'Are you satisfied with the way the game is spreading among the black community?'

'Yes, I am. Cricket is not like other quick games. Even in soccer it does take time to develop a good player, but much more so in regard to cricket. You've got to start playing it when you're young, and we are happy with the programme that the Sports Commission is running at the moment to try to develop cricket in the high-density areas, in the secondary schools and elsewhere.'

'And you've taken the example of Ali Bacher in South Africa. Has that been a help to you?'

'Yes, it is a tremendous help. We would want also to follow what South Africa is doing. They are more advanced there than we are. They started playing cricket ages ago.'

'Where did your own personal love of cricket come from, Sir?'

'Well, I developed the interest at college, not as a player, but as an admirer.'

'You've never played it yourself?'

'No, never. I held a bat once or twice.'

'I'm sure the umpire didn't give you out lbw, did he?'

'Oh, no,'

'But your great love was tennis, wasn't it?'

'Yes, sure, I played tennis, but just for enjoyment.'

'Do you still play occasionally?'

'No. I have a tennis racquet and also two tennis courts, but I have no time for it.'

'Oh dear. You don't look at your racquet wistfully and summon the Minister of Sport and tell him he's got to play a few sets with you?'

'In fact I have yet to answer the challenge from former president Banana. He plays quite often, but I have not been able to do so.'

'I think the Centre Court at Wimbledon should be the venue for that contest. Thank you very much indeed, Sir.' And Henry and I leave the President to the questioning of the newspapers. Needless to say, Blowers is subject to much ribbing for the rest of the day about his closeness to his old friend, Mr Mugabe.

DL

After Henry has grilled the President, we line up in the lunch interval to be presented to him in front of the pavilion. By that time we have taken the lead before Nick Knight has had an unfortunate dismissal. He has edged the leg spinner, Strang, on to the shin of the wicket-keeper and it bounced to first slip. He and Stewart have put on 68 together.

After lunch we also lose Nasser Hussain, driving Strang straight to short extra cover. That brings the two Surrey lads together and they do us proud.

PB

They have taken it to 137 for 3 at tea, which is comparatively good news on which to welcome my teatime visitor to the box. After 'Test Match Special' listeners have heard Henry's interview with Mr Mugabe, I am able to say, 'And from one man of power to another, the Chief Executive of the Test and County Cricket Board, soon to become the England and Wales Cricket Board, Tim Lamb.'

We discuss the changes to the board and whether the new structure can help English cricket on the field. While Tim is an old friend, during the lunch interval, with the rest of the press corps, I have met for the first time the Board's new chairman, Lord MacLaurin. I have been impressed. The chairman of the Tesco supermarket chain, he is talking of making cricket more business-like, of changes to many of the old ways in the current structure. The decline is not cyclical, he insists. 'There are fundamental flaws that we simply have to put right.'

There are signs that these two men at the top of English cricket have been rather shocked by some things in their few days here so far. However, England are still by no means without a chance of winning this Test.

DL

Alec Stewart is in good touch but he's a touch-and-timing player and this is not an ideal pitch for that. Graham Thorpe is out of sorts and looking for touch. But now we've got a partnership. The one thing I've talked about in coaching is partnerships; you've got to put partnerships together. Well, Stewart gets a hundred and Thorpe gets fifty. That is our best partnership so far, and they've put on 106 for the fourth wicket by the end of the day.

It is Alec's first hundred as a wicket-keeper and that's important for him. It just lays that problem to bed for a while. I think we got it right in the way that we jigged the batting order. Alec used to open if he felt like it and he hadn't kept wicket for a long time. If he didn't open, Nick

Knight would have to go from six to one. 'Oh, Nick, you're opening now.'

Alec is happy with the gamble that he might be in after one ball, but if they play properly he's going to get a sit-down and a cup of tea and relax. Everybody has agreed, then, with Hussain coming in at four and Thorpe at five. The key is Crawley at six. You think of Steve Waugh at six for Australia and in the past Clive Lloyd at six for the West Indies. A top player coming in at six. That's great if you can play with the tail and the tail can play with you.

That Stewart and Thorpe partnership has got us into an excellent position. We are 130 on with only three wickets down and they've bowled a lot of overs. You can tell that they're feeling it. So now, as we look forward to the last day, we are hoping to score another hundred with these seven wickets in hand as quickly as possible and look to leave a target of 220 or 230 in sixty overs on a pitch which will be wearing. And it is spinning, and I think our spinners – particularly Croft – are spinning it more than their leg spinner. Croft has never failed to spin it – at good pace.

That is the plan. But again it rains in the evening and throughout the night, and in the morning the ground is soaked. By lunchtime the game is off. Both sides are talking a good game. But we would be setting the declaration. Alistair Campbell would be honour-bound on his home ground to go for whatever it might be. It's a slow outfield, big boundary, the spinners would be calling the tune and Gough, having really hit his straps in the first innings, would also be a handful. Mullally has also continued to trouble them with his angle and his swing. We feel we had a good chance of winning. It is not certain, but we had a good chance. Alistair Campbell is saying, 'We would have gone for them.' That would have helped us.

PB

In the event, when we arrive the ground is saturated. The groundsman has compensated with his covers employed over the suspect ends of the square at the expense of a large area half-way down it. Although we wait through a morning to see if this patch will dry enough to start, it becomes obvious that it will not. Anyway, an hour or so after the match is abandoned, it starts to rain again and does so on and off for the rest of the day.

One other surprise awaits us. Alec Stewart has made a fine undefeated 101, the only century of the match, quite apart from taking a couple of catches and letting through no byes, but the managing director of the firm sponsoring the Test Match, himself a former Zimbabwean player, chooses Grant Flower as Man of the Match for his painstaking 73.

There is one notable achievement to be recorded for Alec Stewart, though. Left out of the first Test of the English summer, following a disappointing tour of South Africa, and written off by some as being at the end of his Test career, he has come back not only to command a certain place in the side, but to score more Test runs in 1996 than any other player in the world – 793. It is a great testimony to his determined spirit.

I find myself feeling for Jack Russell. The principal argument against Stewart keeping wicket for England has been that it affects his batting adversely. So his first hundred as a wicket-keeper is bad news for Jack. He has been a frequent visitor to the 'Test Match Special' box. Something of a tea addict, he has, I think, been more attracted by the size of the teapot that our excellent waiter, Samson, produces regularly than by the quality of our commentary.

The Test series has ended and the commentary team gathers in the evening for dinner together, with some of the people who have helped us. 'Test Match Special' will resurface in about three weeks from New Zealand, and in the meantime Zimbabwe and England have to finish their one-day series. Surely England can demonstrate superiority in those two games.

9

GREAT ZIMBABWE

DAVID LLOYD
With the second one-day international being played on New
Year's Day, we do our celebrating of the New Year twenty-
four hours early. We have a very convivial New Year's Eve
Eve. We're down to work on the next afternoon in a practice
session, though there has been some time for recreation.

Our so-called technical adviser, Mr Ian Botham, has
organised a Ryder Cup-style golf event. The England team
against Sky Television. Beefy sorts it all out – clubs, course,
the lot. I'm paired with Darren Gough, who hits it a country
mile, but unfortunately all over the place and we often can't
find it. If he hit it straight, he would out-drive Ernie Els and
anybody else that plays the game. But we win hands down.
Everybody's elated with that except Botham. So we've got a
win under our belts.

Meanwhile Jack Russell, who's been such a professional
on the tour – because it's not his fault that he's not been
playing – decides he wants to photograph an elephant. He
wants to paint it. So he books in, with Chris Silverwood and
Nick Knight, to go to a nearby game park. Apparently
there's an elephant somewhere there. I say, 'Jack, you're
going to a zoo. It's a zoo, Jack.'

'No,' he says. 'It's a game park.'

When he gets there, he hears that they've found the
elephant, so he takes advice from the wardens on how to

approach it. It seems that they've built a protective barricade so that he can creep up on it from downwind. He has to keep checking the wind, so that the elephant doesn't smell him, but if it does spot him and charges, he's got to run in a zig-zag to the barricade, to confuse the elephant, because it's a bit cumbersome. They don't take prisoners, these elephants.

It takes him ages to get into the strategic position to take his photographs. He's checking the wind and he's creeping slowly nearer and at last he's only five yards away and taking the pictures. Suddenly he sees a fellow walk up to the elephant, carrying a bucket of swill, and pat it on the trunk. This is its dinner. It's called Rosie and it's a tame elephant.

Jack says afterwards, 'I thought I was being so brave.' Well, he was. He didn't know it was domesticated.

New Year's Eve is a quiet night for us, so you hear comments like, 'Here I am, reading a book, having a cup of Horlicks and it's New Year's Eve. Nine or ten o'clock I'm off to bed.' But we're here to work and it's a big game tomor-row. We need to win this game to draw level in the series, to give us a chance to win it in the final game on Friday.

PETER BAXTER

Unlike Christmas on tour, the press party never in my expe-rience seem to have got themselves well organised for New Year's Eve. In the last few years, too, as the size of the party has expanded, we have become more factional, with small tight-knit groups sticking often exclusively together and wary of others who look like breaking into their cliques. That seems a pity on a night like this, but, after packing Henry Blofeld off to see his New Year in at 30,000 feet on his flight home, I welcome 1997 with Edward Bevan and am happy to persuade a Welshman that the Scottish wine is the only one to quaff for Hogmanay.

DL

We've decided that we need six bowlers for the one-dayers here, so we include both Irani and White and there's no room for Graham Thorpe, which is a pity, because he was just showing a bit of touch with that fifty in the second innings of the Test. But we feel that is a balanced one-day side.

We put them in to bat and they commit a bit of hara-kiri and come at it rather like a bull at a gate, so in the tenth over they've lost four wickets for 38, and they're four of the best wickets; Mullally has bowled Waller in the first over, middle stump out, swinging across the line, Hussain's taken a low catch at cover off Gough to get rid of Grant Flower, Houghton has skied Mullally to short mid-wicket and Gough's had Campbell caught behind.

But Craig Evans, who we've come to know and love, because he's spent some time with us, and who's a wonderful golfer, comes together with Andy Flower, who's a stubborn player. He sells his wicket dearly and he's well organised. They put on 59 for the fifth wicket in 13 overs, but we break that stand when Croft has Evans lbw, sweeping, for 32. Guy Whittall is run out by Hussain's throw and Atherton picks up Paul Strang at backward short leg off Croft and it's 126 for 7 in the thirty-third over. We're right on top.

They do bat right down the order, though, and Heath Streak comes in at nine. He and Andy Flower get them out of jail a bit with a stand of 74 in 15 overs. At last Flower skies Mullally, and Gough finishes off the last two. So they're bowled out inside 49 overs for exactly 200. They have been helped a bit by 24 extras, of which 13 are wides and no balls. That's two extra overs bowled.

PB

In the interval between innings it rains. The re-start is delayed by forty-five minutes. This is a moment for which several of us have been waiting – ever since, two or three days before departure, we were sent several pages outlining the 'Duckworth/Lewis method' of deciding a target in these matches. There are several charts, with the aim of making the game fairer than the more familiar and straightforward process of simply applying a faster run rate. This method does make allowance for the fact that, in circumstances like these, the side batting second still has all its wickets to chase a reduced target in fewer overs.

I have asked David Lloyd on the eve of the match if he understood the principles of Duckworth/Lewis. 'No,' he said, 'but I know a man who does.' That man is the England scorer, Malcolm Ashton, who has not even been given as much notice as we have of these charts. His copy arrived on the day he left England. But he has his computer and so, when all eyes turn to him, he is able to say that the target is 185 in 42 overs. (In fact, next day comes news from Lord's that the computed target has to be exceeded, so England should need 186 to win. It's a complicated game at times.)

DL

So we have to score at a faster rate than they did. But it's fairer to both sides, and we're trying the plan and we'll see how it goes.

Nick Knight has the role of attacking in the first fifteen overs, when the field has to be in, but this time it doesn't work and after ten balls he is caught at mid-off for nought off Eddo Brandes. But then Stewart and Crawley get us into a very strong position, putting on 66 in the next ten overs. We lose Stewart, caught behind off Whittall, and then grind to a halt.

You can just see the game going away from us. From a very comfortable four an over, it's gone up to six an over, then seven an over, eight an over. And you're powerless. You're just sitting there and you know that it's just going away. We finish up wanting sixteen off the last over and never in your wildest dreams would you see a county side get themselves into that position in a limited-over competition. We lose the game and we deserve to lose it. So we've lost the series. Inevitably we're going to get some stick. Quite right. That's how it should be.

We have to regroup and, doing my job, there are harsh

words in the dressing room. Short and sharp. That's our business. It's our dressing room.

PB

We onlookers are rather mystified by this failure. It is hard to believe that England's national side appeared to lose its collective bottle. John Crawley has played well for his 73, but he needed to stay there when the run rate required had escalated, and Atherton hitting a long hop straight to long on when he was on 25 was the beginning of the end. They were already needing six an over at that point and Crawley's departure, getting an inside edge on to his foot to be stumped, was the final straw. The penultimate over, bowled by Heath Streak with 19 needed, produces just three runs and brings the wicket of White to drive the message home.

At the post-match press conference, a deflated Atherton pays tribute to a fine Zimbabwean one-day side, and it does seem that few have noticed that they are also now a very experienced one-day international side. Only Alec Stewart has played more matches than any of this opposition. However, everyone knows that the morning's papers at home will dwell not on the virtues of the Zimbabweans, but on the shortcomings of England. That is in the nature of things. David Lloyd, sitting beside Atherton, is forced to admit, rather damningly, that England 'were not up for it'. I can see the pens scurrying over notepads at that piece of modern idiom that seems to suggest an astonishing lack of commitment to the cause.

I put it to Alistair Campbell afterwards that he and his side have sent a message to the cricketing world to take Zimbabwe seriously. 'I've tried to portray that message quite a few times to people,' he says. 'We play a lot of our cricket away from home in tough places like the Indian sub-continent, so we learn the hard way. We can play cricket. We have got people who can compete at the highest level. We have got gifted players and if people want to take us lightly, that's their business.' He sounds confident, too, about taking the series three-nil with another win the day after tomorrow.

DL

I'm a great believer that you should come off the field after a one-day match physically and mentally drained, which they have done, so on the one day in between these two one-day internationals I give them a day off. It lets them re-group. They have leisure time in the morning. I play golf with Beefy again and thoroughly enjoy it, although it has been an effort to do it in the morning. I am glad I have made that effort, because we have a lovely time. Then I have a round of meetings in the afternoon. That's how I spend my day off, talking to various people, some of them press and radio interviews.

My five o'clock meeting is with the players, when again everything is spelt out. The same team is selected, for them to retrieve the situation and get some self-respect. I say that the second part of the tour starts tomorrow, not in New Zealand. We have a full and frank discussion and it's left to the players to put things right in this final one-day inter-national the next day.

PB

On the same evening I am taking part in a forum organised by the former Leicestershire player and now umpire, Barry Dudleston. He has also persuaded the Zimbabwe coach and former captain, David Houghton, to come. He is in splendid form as he gets the opportunity to spell out his vision of the way forward for Zimbabwean cricket. He likes the scene of the small clubs in a place like Barbados, where a simple little ground has its rolled pitch and a pavilion that is little more than a hut, and from that the local community organises its own cricket and starts young players on a trail that can quite easily lead to the island team and then the West Indian team. That, he feels, is the level of encouragement that the Zimbabwe Cricket Union should aim at, spreading the game across a broad base here and building on the exposure that they have gained – especially with a measure of success – to get people organising their own cricket. Small local grounds with a hut and some basic equipment would be the catalyst.

Houghton's words and his obvious commitment to this cause impress the audience of those who have travelled with Barry Dudleston. The future of the game here does so evidently depend on winning the imagination of the majority black population.

Now it is 3 January and, after six weeks in Zimbabwe, this is our last day's cricket. It's the twelfth day the BBC team have witnessed from our elevated little wooden hut, which has now been painted black for the one-day internationals with the coloured clothes and white balls. For today's pitch we are right in line with the wickets, so we are effectively part of the sightscreen. It gives us a chance to rib Geoff Boycott. 'Sit down, Geoffrey. You're holding the game up – again.'

I am a little surprised to read in the local paper of 'the BBC's continued arrogance in describing Zimbabwe as "a team of bits-and-pieces players"'. Asking around, it seems that none of us has actually said that, although bits-and-pieces players are usually just what is required for one-day cricket and Zimbabwe are rather good at it. There is a certain readiness to be insulted overseas that will not be denied and seems to rally a defiant response to what may well be an imagined affront.

We hear that of the replica one-day shirts being sold round the ground the red Zimbabwean ones have sold out, while the light blue England ones have been reduced to half price.

There is one serious note of sadness, too. England take the field wearing black armbands, following the news from Australia that the Surrey wicket-keeper, Graham Kersey, has been killed in a car crash in Brisbane. He was only twenty-five, with a very promising career just burgeoning, and it is clear that the two Surrey players in the side in particular,

Alec Stewart and Graham Thorpe, are very upset at this news. Cricket is a close-knit family and feels such tragedy.

DL

We win the toss again in the morning, and on a dampish sort of pitch, with the possibility of rain around, we invite the opposition to bat. They play well. They play as you'd expect a good one-day team to play – full of inventiveness and flair and imagination.

After we've run out Waller in the fifteenth over for 19, Campbell joins Grant Flower in a second-wicket stand of 73 in fourteen overs. White gets Flower caught at long off for 62, but he's replaced by his brother, who gets 35 in about thirty balls, which just accelerates the innings, and Campbell is 80 not out at the end of the fifty overs. We need 250 to win.

In the interval the 'Cat' meets his leopard. The television people have decided to get hold of it for some feature shots and there it is on a chain-leash on the boundary. So Tuffers goes across to meet it, and he's a bit wary about giving the thing a stroke on the head. It's a beautiful beast.

This target is not beyond us. We are saying to ourselves that this is a better pitch than we've yet seen. 'Come on, boys. There's the challenge. Let's go and knock 'em off.'

Eddo Brandes gives us a lesson in line-and-length seam and swing bowling. He bowls beautifully.

PB

It starts with the last ball of the third over, when Brandes has Nick Knight caught behind down the leg side. Off the first ball of his next over, he has Crawley lbw, coming across his stumps, and Hussain is caught behind first ball to give the man known to all the British tabloids as 'the big chicken farmer' a hat-trick. England are 13 for 3 in the fifth over.

Brandes gets the next two wickets, too. After Stewart and Atherton, who is batting again at five, have clawed together a stand of 32 he has each of them caught behind. At 54 for 5 in the seventeenth over an embarrassing annihilation is an inevitability. It is even more inevitable when Streak gets into the action with the wickets of Irani, caught at cover point, and White, who gives Andy Flower his fifth catch behind the stumps, both of them out without scoring. 63 for 7 in the twentieth over. Though Croft and Mullally offer some sort of resistance with England's highest stand – 41 for the ninth wicket – when Silverwood is out for the fifth duck of the innings, the agony is over. All out in thirty overs for 118. Zimbabwe have won by 131 runs.

DL

It has been a wonderful piece of bowling by Brandes. He's taken 5 for 28 in his ten overs. I'm very pleased for him. It's not so pleasing for our lads, who are on the thick end of it. We have given an abysmal performance, with no major effort other than that 30 not out from Robert Croft at the end.

The team are devastated. You just can't describe it. The work that we've put in; the effort that's gone into it. To perform as we have done in these three one-day internationals leaves us open for so much criticism, which we've just got to take on the chin.

PB

It is a euphoric local crowd that gathers in front of the pavilion to hail the red-shirted Zimbabwean team as they spray champagne from the balcony. The cricket community here is quite small, so it's a club atmosphere as the players call out to friends in the crowd, who toast them back with the songs of celebration. 'Olé, olé, olé, olé. . .' Young girls are tossing bunches of flowers up to the large figure of Craig Evans, who looks an unlikely recipient of a posy. Then they start to chant, 'We want Lloyd, we want Lloyd.' The remarks after Bulawayo are far from forgotten. But Bumble earns a cheer as he appears arm-in-arm with a couple of the home players. Mike Atherton gives a level-headed interview to television up on that same balcony, before coming down to face the press and radio.

I lead off the questioning as usual and find him in a positive frame of mind, but quick to give due praise to the victorious Zimbabweans.

'It's a big defeat and I'd say it's testament to a really good spell of outswing bowling. When a guy gets a hat-trick and you lose 3 for 13 it makes life difficult, and obviously there's no point in just hanging round and using up the overs, you've got to go down with guns blazing and that makes the margin of defeat bigger.

'It's disappointing to lose the one-dayers three-nil. Obviously we would have preferred to have won them. I think the tour can be split very definitely between the one-day games and the Test Matches, where I felt we had the upper hand. In the one-day games we struggled. Zimbabwe have got a good one-day outfit.

'Lots of kind of "bits-and-pieces" cricketers who bat and bowl. They bat all the way down. They've got plenty of options. They've probably got no equals in the field. That makes life difficult. But we've got five one-day games in New Zealand. We'll probably think about our strategy a little bit, maybe change one or two things and hope to perform well there.

'It's fortunate for us that this leg of the tour's over. Things have declined a little bit in this game. It's nice just to have a break and go to a new venue, where players can pick themselves up and aim for a very successful second leg, and that's what we aim to do.

'I don't think the team will need raising. They're very disappointed. I'm disappointed. But nobody's downhearted. We know that we've got the second leg of the tour coming up. There's no point in crying over spilt milk. We've got to get on with it and work hard at our game and hope to put things right in the second leg and that's what we're intending to do. I don't see any point in either me or the players giving up.'

The England team have witnessed the captain's performance on television and, after that, he is welcomed back into the dressing room by a round of applause from his men.

DL

I'll just be defiant in saying that the Test Matches have simply disappeared. That seems ages ago. We were the dominant team in both Test Matches, but we're leaving here as failures, because we've lost the one-day international series three-nil. We have never been guilty of underestimating the opposition. I don't know where that idea has come from. I don't know how people can say that, because of the planning that we've put into it. In the final analysis in the one-day competition we were just not up to it. We were nowhere near as good as they were. They were a vibrant team, just the type of team that we're looking to be. One-day cricket is different. This is the England that came back from South Africa and the World Cup having had a dreadful time. We picked different teams for the one-day internationals against India and Pakistan, two top sides, and we just dominated both series. We played exceptionally well, with flair, imagination, know-how and a lot of intelligence. The lads on this tour have an opportunity and a challenge to get into one-day cricket and to play it as it should be played. Now, against Zimbabwe, we have just not done it. The game is not played on paper and it's not about comparing man for man. It's a collective team effort. We didn't show the necessary flair and vibrancy in any department and we've paid the price. We've lost.

This evening there is a farewell cocktail party for the team. I am delayed setting off from our hotel, having to do some press interviews. Wayne Morton is waiting for me and for Alec Stewart, who had to make some phone calls. The party is being held at the National Brewery, so we get directions from Bernard Chimanga, the man on the front desk at the hotel, though we are not holding our breath that he has sent us to the right place.

He has said it will take us ten minutes and, sure enough,

Mayhem in Mashonaland. Nasser Hussain is bowled by James Kirtley as England go down to an unexpected defeat. (*Allsport*)

In the nets at Bulawayo. Darren Gough, Robert Croft and friend *(Allsport)*; Geoffrey Boycott shows Mike Atherton how to play a straight bat *(Peter Baxter)*.

The first one-day international at Bulawayo. Darren Gough appeals in vain for the wicket of Guy Whittall; Mike Atherton hits out, and is caught. *(Allsport)*

The dramatic First Test at Bulawayo. Robert Croft gets the wicket of Andy Waller.
Below: Nasser Hussain and John Crawley both got centuries in England's first innings.
(Allsport)

England coach David Lloyd, with Ian Botham *(Allsport)*.

The BBC commentary team at Bulawayo: *from left,* Chris Cowdrey, Trevor Bailey, Henry Blofeld, Simon Mann, Jo King. *Right:* Peter Baxter adjusts the commentary rota. *(Peter Baxter)*

Paul Strang, who took seven wickets for
Zimbabwe in the Bulawayo Test.
(Allsport)

Heath Streak commiserates with Nick
Knight as the First Test ends with scores
level. *(Allsport)*

The Second Test at Harare. David Houghton (*above*)
and Zimbabwe captain Alistair Campbell. (*Allsport*)

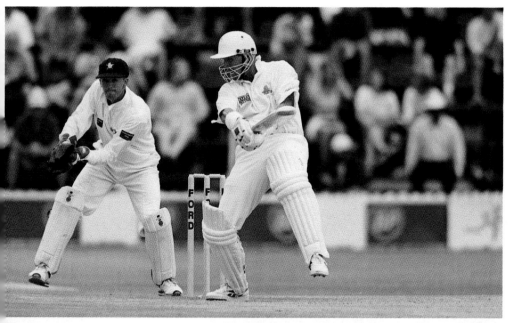

Alec Stewart on his way to a century at Harare – then the rains came.
(*Allsport*)

Jack Russell had plenty of time to paint on this tour, here at the grave of Cecil Rhodes. England scorer Malcolm Ashton looks on. (*Peter Baxter*)

The teams line up for the second one-day international. England in blue – which matched their mood at the end. (*Allsport*)

after ten minutes we see a tower carrying the words 'HARARE BREWERY'. So we turn into this yard. There is the security guard, dressed like Fireman Sam, with overalls and a helmet and the customary boots with no laces. He's got a big smile on his face. I do the talking. 'We're with the England cricket team. We've come to the cocktail party. Sorry we're a little bit late, we just got delayed. Where are the team? The England cricket team?'

'Yes,' he says, 'Oh yes.'

'Where are they?'

'Oh yes. Team.'

'Yes. Where are they? It's a cocktail party.'

'Yes.'

'Well, could you tell us where to go, please?'

'Left.'

'Thank you.' Off we go, driving round the building, and there are barrels and crates and pallets. It's getting dingier and dingier. We go round in a full circle. He's there again.

'We can't actually find them. Can you tell us again where they are? The England cricket team for the cocktail party. The farewell from the Zimbabwe Cricket Union.'

'Yes. Oh yes.'

'Where can we park?'

'Park here, yes.'

So we park. 'Have you got a reception area?'

'Oh yes.' So we get to the reception area and it's the same story. There's a fellow in a cap.

'We're from the England cricket team and we've come to the cocktail party. Now, where are they? We can't seem to find them.'

'Oh dear.'

Then, with a stroke of genius, I ask him, 'This is the National Brewery, isn't it?'

'No.'

It turns out the National Brewery is three miles down the road. We set off, past the original security man. He's got a big beam on his face. I stop and say to him, 'The bomb that

I've planted is just round the corner next to the barrels. It'll go up with a hell of a bang. We'll just go to the cocktail party and we'll come back with a couple of brushes and shovels and sweep it up when we leave. Is that all right?'

'Yes. Oh yes.'

It was farewell to Zimbabwe, where we have had one or two communication problems.

10

PARTING THOUGHTS

PETER BAXTER

It is Saturday, 4 January and in the foyer of the Monomatapa
Hotel in Harare the England team's huge cricket cases are
lined up for loading on to the transport to the airport. At
mid-day they will be on their way to Johannesburg on the
first leg of the long, wearying journey to New Zealand. I will
not be with them, so this is the time for thanks and good-
byes.

I am taking the opportunity to see this magnificent country. My wife is arriving and we will embark on a memorable
trip round the Eastern Highlands, the ancient and mysterious buildings of Great Zimbabwe, Hwange National Park,
Victoria Falls and Lake Kariba. Throughout our tour,
though, we will inevitably be greeted by smiles of triumph
from our Zimbabwean hosts.

The old lion has been humbled. Any performances in the
Tests are largely forgotten. The one-day internationals
happened last and therefore grabbed the headlines. They
were conclusive and the Tests were not. No matter that one
more ball might have brought an England win in Bulawayo.
It did not, and the Zimbabweans were triumphant in their
defiance. At least that is how it has been painted, for it is
certain that Zimbabwe have won the public relations battle.

On this front England have – not for the first time – been
surprisingly naive. It was obvious early on that Alistair

93

Campbell particularly seems very adept at playing up the perception of what he described as England's 'superiority complex'. It is just the sort of fodder to gee up his team. Make the visitors appear the arrogant colonial power, and we are the slightly cheeky, irreverent and infinitely more straightforward and trustworthy country cousins who will just show them a thing or two. The Australian publicity machine has been playing the same game for years, and nowadays every Ashes series is marketed there along those lines.

It is a difficult attitude to counter and made more so with a few propaganda gifts. The 'We murdered them' quote was obviously one of those, and Mike Atherton's apparently sullen and sulky body language was another. A few other grains of truth were cleverly worked on. We were told that the England team never had a drink with their opposite numbers. There may well have been truth in that on some days, because there is inevitably a difference in approach by English players to what is for them a full-time job from that of Zimbabwe's players, even those for whom cricket is now a full-time profession. They are at home, in many cases playing on their own club ground with the crowd containing a large proportion of their friends and fellow club members. The incentive of the post-match drink is greater for them.

A source who should have known assured me that there was a lot of sledging going on in the middle and that it all came from England. English sources told me that it was fairly even – and the evidence of my eyes, watching moving lips through binoculars, seemed to confirm that.

I have, though, believed for some time that England make bad tourists because of a subconscious underestimation of many of their opponents. They are bound to deny it, but I feel I have often witnessed an unstated attitude of 'We are the professionals here. We do this job seven days a week, you're just playing it as a game.' Add to that the Englishman's inbred assumption of superiority over all foreigners (if they don't understand English, just talk louder) and a rather contradictory impression that to adopt

94

the patriotic attitudes which seem to come more naturally to newer countries is not very 'cool' for an Englishman, and you have a recipe for overseas embarrassment.

Lord MacLaurin and the ECB will be considering the whole structure of English cricket, which always seems to happen when England have a less than successful series. My own preference – and, as a traditionalist, I am a devotee of county championship cricket – is for a two-division championship. The resurgence in English rugby seems to date from the introduction of the league divisions in the club game. The cream is then allowed to rise more naturally. It would very probably lead to a more vigorous transfer system, but if that is the price for improving the England team it is a necessary one to pay. It might just provide added vitality to the Championship anyway.

Here, perhaps, England were on a hiding to nothing. No less than a resounding victory was expected – demanded, even – by the home public. If the Test Match performances have been dogged by some bad luck – and, it must be said, sessions of indifferent performance, which meant having to make up ground from behind – the failures in the one-day internationals were astonishingly comprehensive, to the mystification of many onlookers of both sides.

It is so often said that England's players play so much one-day cricket that they must be experts. Indeed, in at least one of these games here – possibly all three – one would have expected a county side to have beaten Zimbabwe from the same position. Although there is a great deal of county one-day cricket played, England play fewer one-day internationals than any other top-flight cricket country.

I am not the greatest fan of one-day international cricket and that appears to be the majority British reaction. Other countries place far greater store on these contests, not least because in their home lands this is the greatest source of revenue for the game. Specially selected one-day sides at home have performed well for England. They have been to three World Cup Finals, two of them abroad, but I wonder, when they haul on the coloured uniforms now demanded in almost every other country for limited-over cricket, does their subconscious tell them that these clown costumes make it not quite the real thing? Does a little voice say, 'This is a pantomime costume for an afternoon's family entertainment and the result doesn't really matter'? I hasten to say that if you see the disappointment after a failure this attitude is not evident. Still, as I am not sure that I do not harbour it somewhere at the back of my own mind, maybe it also lodges deeper in the players.

One-day international cricket may just be rather like the European Community. We don't really like it and it's not very British, but we are in it, so to do well in it we must grasp it with both hands. Perhaps we should don the coloured clothing for home internationals. Before you recoil with horror, let me say that I am right beside you. Personally, I dislike coloured clothing for daytime cricket. It is essential for the night game, of course, and adds to a thrilling – but totally different – spectacle. But if we are to join in the general opprobrium heaped on the England team for one-day failures, it may be that, as an indication that we take this different form of the game seriously and that we do think it matters, the time has come to take the international consensus view on 'pyjamas'.

It has become the accepted way – not just in cricket – to blame the press. The British public does not have a very high regard for the press itself – it says. However, they do seem to believe it and to adopt its view, and victories over the press are pretty scarce. It is a battle – sometimes of their own invention – that our cricketers are unlikely to win, so maybe a more pragmatic approach is required.

I have said that the England players are a bit naive about public relations. It might help them to be more aware of what it is that each writer or broadcaster is after. Attempts to score points off them usually rebound. More difficult to tame are the photographs. The players have a generally good relationship with the photographers on a tour, but I have often been shocked to read, on my return from a tour, the sometimes unfair and frequently downright inaccurate captions given – presumably by a sub-editor in London – to some pictures published in the papers.

The 1993 tour of India was a classic illustration of this, when players were castigated on a daily basis for being scruffy, without any explanation of the often quite reasonable circumstances of that scruffiness. The very popular manager, Bob Bennett, was a victim of that. Players were depicted sweating on the training ground with the implication in the caption that this was how they presented themselves in the streets of Delhi. A picture was published of the team's arrival in Calcutta for the First Test. They were wearing tracksuits. What a way to present yourselves for such a big occasion, you might think. What was not fully explained was that it was five o'clock in the morning and they had gone straight from a match in Cuttack to a nine-hour train journey on bunks that were more like shelves. They looked a good deal smarter than those of us who had accompanied them in the same sleeper coach. We can blame the sub-editors for some of that, but the photographers themselves know that if England are losing, a shot of the manager blinking will do very nicely for a caption, 'He can't bear to watch'. In those circumstances I do sympathise with the players. We need some integrity.

Of course, particularly against supposedly weak opposition, defeat attracts bigger headlines than victory. 'PLUCKING USELESS' to accompany the tale of chicken farmer Brandes's deeds, 'SPINELESS' or 'IT DOESN'T GET ANY WORSE THAN THIS' lodge in the players' minds and lead to their accusation that the media are only happy when England lose. The style of some writers, it is true, may well be more suited to accounts of disaster than success, but I simply do not believe that any of them want England to lose.

Certainly the public at home do not. What filters through to us speaks of a more extreme reaction there than those of us on the spot are immediately aware of. I have noticed this on past tours, both in victory and defeat. Thus on the morning of the final one-day international comes the interview question from London, 'Will Mike Atherton resign before the New Zealand leg of the tour?'

'No,' I reply, quite shocked. 'Of course not.'

'Why not?' is the aggressively put response.

'He's in the middle of the tour. And, frankly, it is not in his character to quit.'

On this departure Saturday I make a particular point of thanking the captain for his help and co-operation. Yes, no matter what you may hear about 'Captain Grumpy', I find Mike Atherton a man of great charm in personal dealings. He is perhaps too careless for his own good of his public image, which is probably one of the things I like about him. I think he would serve himself better if he were not so apparently contemptuous of the press as a group. Individually, he gets on very well with many of them.

He is his own man, who does not suffer fools gladly and sometimes lets that be known. A man of great strength of character, he may have played more of his cricket in pain from his back than he is prepared to admit. It might also explain the folded arms in the field on occasions when more expressive body language seems to be called for. But then he might see that as being just for public consumption and therefore a waste of effort. His team is what matters.

I feel a twinge of regret, as I see them go, that my part in their New Zealand adventure will be through the night from the depths of Broadcasting House. But in the meantime the game parks await.

11

NEW ZEALAND: A CHANGE OF SCENE

JONATHAN AGNEW

When Peter Baxter rang me from Gatwick on 25 November, as England were about to depart for Zimbabwe, I really believed that that part of the tour would be little more than a warm-up for the more serious business which I would attend in New Zealand. How wrong we all have been!

I have found it fascinating being in England, for once, while the cricket team is overseas. It is very easy, as a member of the travelling press corps, to become too embroiled in what is happening on a tour because it is not possible to keep it in perspective along with everything else that is happening in England at the same time. When you are reporting on a cricket tour, nothing else matters and this is made even worse when there is a considerable time difference with England because you have very little personal contact with people in the office. You really do feel that you are on your own.

What has hit me hardest, as England have struggled in Zimbabwe, has been the strength of feeling amongst the cricketing public at home who have been genuinely angry and concerned by the results. There have been phone-ins on radio stations and pages of readers' letters in the newspapers amidst a universal feeling of despair. Some of the reporting by my colleagues in the media was very close to the bone but, after all, it was hardly going to be complimentary, so I have been astonished to learn that copies of newspaper articles have been regularly faxed out to the England team in Zimbabwe. I really think that was utter madness and something which must be addressed on future tours because no one likes to read criticism of their efforts. Although I am sure that the players would admit that they played badly in the one-day internationals in particular, it will not have done them any good at all to have read as much in the match reports.

So the relations between the team and the press hit an all-time low, which was illustrated by the refusal by the players to attend the traditional Christmas drinks party. It seemed to be a terribly sad decision and I was surprised that John Barclay, the tour manager, did not put his foot down and insist that the players go, if only for an hour. The bottom line is that there is not one journalist on the tour who does not want England to win; it is our national team, for goodness sake, and a few of us have actually played for England. Unfortunately, some of the current players appear to believe strongly that the English press gains some kind of macabre satisfaction in watching them lose, which simply is not true. When England begin to play well again and win Test matches, the cricketers will, naturally, notice a huge difference in the coverage they receive in the press.

It would be an interesting exercise for the cricketers, themselves, to sit down in a quiet moment and write an honest account of one of those one-day internationals in order to understand and appreciate for a moment what it is like to be in the other camp.

It has come as no surprise, in the New Year, to read the mounting speculation about Mike Atherton's future as captain. He has not been in the best of form with the bat in Zimbabwe, but I feel that is irrelevant to the captaincy debate. Atherton is a fine player and a man who does not appear to be affected by a lean patch. However, the feeling

100

has seemed to be amongst many of my colleagues who were in Zimbabwe that unless England's fortunes change dramatically in New Zealand there should be a change at the top before the Australians arrive in the summer.

DAVID LLOYD

The journey from Harare to Auckland, with all the time differences, takes about forty hours. We fly from Harare to Johannesburg, have a few hours to wait there, and then Johannesburg to Perth and on to Sydney, where we have a six-hour delay before flying on to Auckland. That is a bit of a nuisance, but it's been a comfortable enough flight and we've slept, played cards and watched several films. We've been able to watch live cricket in various airport lounges – Australia against the West Indies and South Africa against India.

South Africa have been in India on dusty, turning pitches and India have won and now they're straight back to South Africa on the biggest, bounciest things you've ever seen. We're watching the Cape Town Test, where Nelson Mandela comes at lunchtime and all the players are introduced and the interval is extended by a few minutes. I don't know what that did to Tendulkar and Azharuddin, but I wouldn't have missed it for the world. They've come out and it's a shot a ball. Every one's a winner. They clatter a hundred each and it's breathtaking. Great strokeplay. It doesn't matter who comes on to bowl, Donald, Pollock, Klusener, they've all got to go. They were 58 for 5 when these two started together and they're up to 280 in no time, and we are all sat round cheering every shot.

In Sydney we've seen the Australian papers rubbishing the Australian team, which has given us a bit of heart after the pummelling we've had. We say, 'Hello, look at this. Australia have lost ten of the last twelve one-day matches they've played. Their captain hasn't scored a fifty for the last twelve months.' It comes home to us that here is a top side at long last getting some stick from their own media. It takes

101

a bit for their press to get stuck in. I seem to remember that when they went to Pakistan and lost, they came back as national heroes. All the blame was put on Pakistan; they didn't play the game, the pitches weren't right and the food was dreadful. Now there is criticism of the captain at the top of the innings. We are seeing, 'Should he be captain?' We read that Ian Healy has attended a press conference after scoring a hundred and just used it as a platform to bag whoever had written that he was about to lose the vice-captaincy. He got into a bit of trouble for that. It just shows us that you're there to be shot down unless you perform at the highest level.

We are to find a difference in New Zealand, when we beat Northern Districts in two and a half days and the whole tenor of the press is about how well their man Tait has bowled. It's a positive angle, which is a luxury, I think. However, I should say that I enjoy our press conferences and I think they're good. I think we've got decent people. I will give my view and then they ask questions, and I'd say that they are conducted properly. And we do get on.

We arrive in Auckland at 4.30 in the morning and we are bright as buttons. All the changes in times and the amount of sleep we have been able to get mean that we don't want to go to bed. We feel we have to stay awake until the evening. We do as well as we can. We have a press conference at eleven, so straight away we've got to get dressed up. We've got to look the part.

The press conference is conducted very well by the New Zealand Board. It's well orchestrated and structured. There's a lady called Michelle Lewis, who looks after the media side of things here, and she has Martin Crowe leading off. The New Zealand captain, Lee Germon, is on the top table with Mike Atherton and me and the newly appointed New Zealand coach, Steve Rixon. They call for questions.

A fellow stands up in the front row. He looks familiar, but I have not associated the name and the face with cricket. He is an ITN news reporter called Michael Nicholson. He's not a cricket man at all. You usually see him in places like Beirut or Bosnia. Well, he just fires off, asking if the captain is going to do the decent thing and resign. He tells us we're the object of ridicule. You try to pre-empt the questions, but we certainly aren't ready for that lot from a fellow who just doesn't know cricket.

Mike Atherton does really well. One question that Nicholson asks I start to answer, and he says, 'I am not speaking to you.' So I feel honour-bound to say, 'Well, I'm speaking to you.'

Even our press are a bit taken aback at this assault when you're just off a flight and looking to start afresh. We're trying to get through this press conference, but we can never do it because he is on a hatchet job. He's after the captain and the coach, but mainly the captain. Now he follows us round, wanting another England debacle. We are told, though, that he is on stand-by for Boris Yeltsin's condition deteriorating. If it does, he'll have to pop off to Moscow. But he stalks us for a while, though we have no contact. It all seems a bit sad.

We're based in Auckland for our early practice sessions and our first impressions are that it's a lovely place, a clean city with a nice harbour. The management and the team have chatted and said, 'This is a new leg of the tour. You've got a challenge. We've played poorly in one-day cricket. The challenge is that we're going to win everybody round and it starts now. We start afresh.' And I want everybody in the side to relax, to start by getting away from the game and having a look round. We go on a boat trip round the harbour with a lovely barbecue. There are a number of players who want to do that. There's a bit of fishing to be had as well. So we generally relax at this base.

Then we come down to the nets at Eden Park. This is a fresh start in a comfortable environment. More like England, if you like, because we're not at altitude and, whilst it's hot, it's pleasant.

JA

As I begin the mind-numbing journey to New Zealand, I am determined to keep an entirely open mind about Atherton's position, and also that of David Lloyd, the coach, whom I have known for a long time. 'Bumble' has attracted a lot of criticism for his comments after the Bulawayo Test partly because, I believe, he encountered the same reaction as the one I received during the Atherton 'dirt in the pocket affair' three years ago. His outburst greatly surprised people who were used to him being nothing more than a bright and jolly commentator on 'Test Match Special'. He was not expected to voice strong and controversial opinions. There are times when 'Bumble' has to fight hard to keep his emotions under control because he is such an intense, enthusiastic man, and fiercely loyal to his players. It is unfortunate, but inevitable, that his ability as a coach will be judged almost entirely on results, and England's long-suffering supporters are demanding an immediate improvement.

However, the fact is that if England do well in New Zealand, much of the disappointment we all feel about the Zimbabwean leg will diminish dramatically and the pressure will then be off both the captain and the coach, at least for the time being.

DL

After four days, we move on to New Plymouth for a fifty-over game against the New Zealand Cricket Academy. It's a beautiful ground. I played here once with Fred Trueman. It was one of F. S. Trueman's extravaganzas. He got a team together during the Centenary Test in Australia in 1977. It included Ian Botham, Peter Lever and myself. We had Godfrey Evans behind the sticks, Fred opening the bowling, Peter Parfitt in a pair of golf shoes at mid-off and Brian Close. I won the man of the match award for making seventy-odd. I can't even remember who we were playing against, but I won a dozen bottles of champagne. I did a couple of interviews after the game and chatted to a few

104

people, and when I got back into the dressing room they'd supped all the champagne. And they were saying, 'Well done, old boy, it was very pleasant.' So I remember the place. It is a beautiful amphitheatre, Pukekura Park.

We have a little illness in the team in these early days in New Zealand. It's not a big problem. There's a bit of a virus that seems to be going round. There's a bit of sweating, cold, aching. That starts with Hussain and then goes on to White and Caddick and Knight. We've just got to get on with it.

We've also got the cyclone. We've heard a little bit about Cyclone Drena and apparently it's heading our way, so batten down the hatches, because it's going to whizz through. In the event, we just catch the edge of it. It's quite spectacular rain and wind, but nothing like some of the rain we had in Zimbabwe.

We know that this cyclone is about to hit us as we win the toss here in New Plymouth, but we want to field and we get forty overs in. It's a small ground, so we play all the seamers and we particularly want to give Dominic Cork a good bowl – we're glad to see him after he had to miss Zimbabwe. He bowls seven overs and takes one for 39, and we bowl them out for 201. Caddick takes 3 for 44, Silverwood 2 for 32, Gough 2 for 35 and Irani 2 for 49.

Then the cyclone hits, so we don't get the chance to bat, but the great thing is that we've got the bowlers through, which is important after jet-lag and after a relaxing time. You just want to get some overs into their legs. But once the rains come there is no question that we will play again. So we move on to Palmerston North to play against a Select XI.

When we get there we have a look at the ground. We walk on, new to the area, to see what sort of pitch it is, and you're always expecting the groundsman to come and clear you off. Russell Smith is the groundsman. He's a terrific bloke. He's so nice and so polite. 'Of course you can have nets. I'll have them ready for you at a quarter past eight in the morning.' The pitch? Yes, it does this; it does that. 'Can I do anything for you? Do you like fishing? Do you want to borrow my rods? Of course you can play football over there.' I think, crikey, where have you been? This is a different breed. This is a really nice fellow.

It's the best place in the world for fishing in these rivers, so we go big-game fishing, and although we take the Reverend Andrew Wingfield-Digby, the former team chaplain, in the hope of some divine help, we catch nothing. We've even bought licences, so we're not poaching. John Barclay and Athers even go night fishing, but no fish.

It's the usual thing. New Zealand will see this Select XI as a chance for a number of their Test players. Mark Greatbatch is playing with Adam Parore, Craig Spearman, Blair Pocock, Justin Vaughan, Danny Morrison coming back from injury, and Mark Haslam, the left-arm spinner. So they want a strong side out.

We win the toss again and invite the Select XI to bat. It jags around a bit and we bowl them out for 138, with our bowlers bowling really well: Cork, Caddick, Silverwood in particular, and Craig White, bowling ten overs and taking 4 for 15, on a pitch that did a bit. White has bowled quick, into a stiff breeze – somebody had to – and he's bowled some sharp deliveries and they couldn't handle him. It is a good pitch to bowl on, but we have bowled with good discipline, we've bowled patiently, we haven't given anything away, we've been well-focused and that has been very pleasing for me. Everybody has hit his straps and they've worked as a team in the field.

The plan for Craig White now is that we have the option of him as third seamer with two spinners, or fourth with one spinner. But, importantly, he just galvanises the bottom order. I think the theory of having John Crawley at six is terrific, but what we're not doing is giving him support, which we need to do.

The captain's still not getting runs. He's working hard in the nets. I'm trying to work with him, putting sharp spells in with plenty of time in the nets. He's got plenty of people throwing the ball and bowling to him and he gets on the bowling machine. It needs patience from us and patience from him and reminding him that he can play. I get his stats out. 'These are your last eight Test Matches and you're still averaging 35.' I think, no matter who it is, they need reminding. But he's such a hard character. He's still brilliant with his team, caring, not worrying about them but mindful of their needs. If there's somebody a bit down he'll go and knock on his door and sit and spend time with him away from the game. He doesn't shy away from saying, when he needs to, 'Look, I'm not happy with what happened today.' But he himself is not down. He's philosophical about his form. He knows that he's going to get runs and it's with patience that it will come. He certainly doesn't sit around and mope. He joins in with the players and enjoys going off fishing whenever he can, and all the media speculation about whether he will keep the captaincy genuinely doesn't affect him at all. He's written himself that he'd like to captain against Australia in the summer, but will understand that if he doesn't perform someone else will get the job. It's as simple as that. It's the way of the world. He just gets on with his job.

Today he's lbw for 7, but Alec Stewart continues to play magnificently. He plays beautifully, scores 153 and then retires hurt, doing the decent thing and letting somebody else come in to bat. He's had a good partnership with Nasser Hussain, who bats beautifully for 139, and they add 215 together. Eventually we declare at 427 for 8.

Now the Select team have got a lot of work to do to get anywhere near us. We've got a terrific lead of 289. The pitch has flattened out a fair amount, but again we start making inroads and the spinner comes into play – Phil Tufnell. Silverwood picks up wickets again – he gets three for 29 – and Tufnell has five for 58. At the end there's a bit of fun from Danny Morrison, hitting Tuffers for a couple of sixes and making 30, but we bowl them out for 176 and win by an innings and 113 runs.

Again we've bowled well. We've bowled with good

discipline. We've got the thing in the right area. We've also got one magnificent run-out. Jack Russell has been on as substitute fielder, stalking, Jonty Rhodes-style, in the covers. Mark Greatbatch takes a single to him, a very sharp one, and Jack's on it like a flash and throws the stumps down. It should have been a Test Match at the Melbourne Cricket Ground, with 90,000 people to watch him. He's run round the field; he's done high fives with everybody, Alec Stewart's picked him up. It's a great moment – the Champagne Moment of the tour without the champagne. Veuve Clicquot should give him a bottle. If only all players were like him in the professionalism that he shows. He's a credit to his club and to himself. So we're moving on and we're in good form. We're going to Hamilton to play against Northern Districts.

JA

It does not matter how many times you have visited New Zealand before, it is impossible not to be struck by the beauty of the countryside and the warmth of the welcome from the locals. It is often the case these days that hectic tours do not allow time for either the journalists or the crick-eters to see a great deal more than airport lounges, hotels and cricket grounds, so any opportunity to see a bit of the country you are visiting must be eagerly taken.

I have the luxury of a free day in Auckland between arriving and setting off for my first match in Hamilton, so I hire a car and head north to the Bay of Islands. What a glorious drive! The journey there takes three hours and the scenery is breathtaking: rolling, tree-covered hills and deep, green valleys, lakes and, every now and then, a glimpse of the sea. It is also extremely hot, and after a month of virtually non-stop frost in England the weather comes as a pleasant change.

The Bay of Islands is beautiful. It is as it sounds: a series of inlets and bays with rocky islands of various sizes stand-ing out of the sea. It is very similar to the Grenadines in the

West Indies, and I spend an hour wandering about, watching the yachts coming and going before reluctantly starting the return trip to Auckland. Three hundred miles in a day is a good way of defeating jet-lag!

Vic Marks telephones from the hotel reception at seven o'clock the next morning. He has just flown in from London and we have pre-arranged to drive down to Hamilton together. He heads up to my room to freshen up after his flight and, after an interval of three months, it is great to see a familiar figure shuffling down the corridor, dragging his suitcase wearily behind him. I note, as we greet each other, that his favourite old cotton jacket has been brought out for yet another tour.

The journey to Hamilton takes a couple of hours, and Vic and I talk cricket all the way. He appears to be as keen as I am to get working again after a lay-off and, as I settle in at the ground the next morning, I cannot wait for the cricket to start.

DL

We've been hoping to have a look at Simon Doull, the Northern Districts and New Zealand fast bowler, in this match, but he's been pulled out of the game by the New Zealand coach, the Australian, Steve Rixon. He doesn't want England to see Doull. I understand that, but when we get on the pitch we find it's damp and green and Doull's there, so it's crying out for them to say, 'Right, he plays. He could just embarrass England.' That's what I would have said. Let him bowl as many overs as he wants, or as few, but if he's getting wickets he can embarrass the touring team in the last match before the First Test. But they leave him out and they have quite an ordinary attack.

We win the toss, stick them in and bowl them out in a session. Cork three for 18, White three for 17 and Gough three for 23. So all the seamers have done it and we've bundled them out in a session. Cork's bowled straight, with pace, and he's swung it. He's got both the New Zealand Test

109

openers, Young and Pocock, for four and none, so that's a good blow for us. They're 69 all out.

JA

After seeing that, I inform my press colleagues who have been in Zimbabwe that I shall never believe another word they write in the future! Like 'Bumble', I am also surprised that Doull has been left out on such a green pitch. Conversely, Young and Pocock have been allowed to play. It seems to have been the wrong way round, in that Doull might have revelled in the conditions and scored some psychological points against England's batsmen, while the batsmen appear to be on a hiding to nothing.

I have a brief conversation with Doull, who is a very pleasant chap with a goatee beard and two earrings in his left ear. He seems rather frustrated at being left out.

DL

We also find that it's a difficult pitch to bat on. We have to work hard. There are a few runs for Knight and Stewart. Athers is lbw again for 5, walking across the crease. I'm disappointed with that, but they've got a bowling machine and they've got a good indoor shed, so we're in it and doing a lot of work there.

Graham Thorpe had an indifferent time in Zimbabwe, but now he plays well on a pitch that's doing a bit and he and Crawley put a partnership together. Thorpe gets 71 and Crawley 65. Craig White comes in for 22 not out, but we lose the plot and eight, nine, ten, eleven are all out weakly. Still, we've got a big lead of 225.

JA

A 17-year-old left-arm spinner called Daniel Vettori is making his first-class debut for Northern Districts and immediately catches my eye. He is a student, and rather earnestly looks the part with his long brown hair and wire-rimmed, round spectacles. He shows no signs of nerves as

110

he tosses the ball up and finds just enough turn to trouble the batsmen. I spend much of the match commentating on New Zealand Radio Network One, and suggest that this youngster is definitely one for the future. I do not know at the time that he will be called up for the New Zealand Test team just three weeks later after only one more first-class match.

Cork makes such a difference to England. He lifts the whole team with his enthusiasm, not to mention his ability to take wickets, and he is clearly relishing the opportunity to run through the Northern Districts in their second innings. He disposes of the New Zealand opener, Young, for the second time in the match but, having bowled nine overs, he limps off, clutching his back. This creates a sudden flurry of activity in the press box, and this is heightened by the gloomy statement from Wayne Morton, the physiotherapist, who reveals that Cork has felt a sharp, stabbing pain in his back and is struggling to move. With the first Test only five days away, England's most potent weapon is now trussed up in a corset.

The following day, X-rays rule out the threat of any serious structural damage to Cork's back and the worry is that he has suffered a torn muscle. Again, Morton's view does not seem optimistic in the least, and one or two of my colleagues feel obliged to rule Cork out of the Test. Some go even further and write that his tour might very well be over before it has really begun.

DL

It's a good story for the papers, moving it on from Atherton. Cork was feeling sore in the morning and I've been talking up the story that he won't play in the First Test. But he will. I'm doing rather what Lancashire did before the Lord's final with Jason Gallian. 'No, he won't play.' Then name him in the team in the morning. That's the way that I want to do it. With Cork it looks like a soft-tissue strain and should settle down, I hope, in two or three days, and we've got three days

111

before the Test Match. To prove his fitness to me he'll have to bowl a sustained spell in the last net before the match and come away with no effects the following morning. He'll have to be right. If he says, 'I'm 80 per cent fit', he doesn't play.

So now, in Hamilton, it's Mullally who really hits his straps on a pitch that has flattened out. He takes four, White gets a couple and Gough comes in with some pace and a bit of fire-power and slips three out, and we've bowled them out for 259 on a flat pitch.

We need 35 to win and obviously the story for the papers would be if Athers gets out cheaply again. He could say, 'Goughie, get yourself in there', but he goes in to face the new ball. He's only got 12 not out when we win by ten wickets, but he wants a bit of time in the middle and that will have done him the world of good, because he's a strong character.

JA

Understandably, there is some speculation about whether or not Atherton will open the innings. It seems that he is on a hiding to nothing in that, at best, he could score fifteen or twenty runs; at worst he could fail again. However, Atherton is nothing if not extremely determined and it is no surprise to me that he strides out to bat with Knight and finishes not out. England win their second first-class match on the New Zealand leg by ten wickets with a day and a quarter to spare and, apart from Cork's injury, their visit to Hamilton has been a highly profitable one.

DL

Before we've finished in Hamilton, we get to know that New Zealand are going to play a two-day, one-innings-per-side game in Auckland. So I leave our team and drive up there to watch the game. It's on their second pitch – what a facility. It's brilliant. There's no secrecy about it. I just walk straight in and set my camera up. They give me lunch. There are a few jokes about 'You're a spy', and a young lady from a TV station says, 'Is this cricket?'

I say, 'Oh, I think so. Steve Rixon, the New Zealand coach has been watching us in Palmerston North and Hamilton and I'm watching his team now.' I don't see a problem there. It gives me the chance to see Simon Doull, who's been hidden from us. So now I've got some film of him and we can plug it into the video in our team-room and have a look at him. I know, from being an opening batsman myself, that you want to have seen a bowler before you face him in the middle. It's dreadful to face someone you've never seen before. You've got to know just how he runs up and where he runs from. How does he bowl from the crease? Is he wide; is he close; what's his follow-through like? It's the bowler you've never seen – no matter how poor he may be – that's the danger.

In fact, New Zealand bat first and the top four get rolled over by Auckland. I've still not seen Brian Young get past the first over. Nathan Astle scores runs, but he scores them airborne. He doesn't like it short. He slaps it into the covers head-high. He drives on the up, lays shots and likes hitting fours. It's the first time I've seen Lee Germon, the captain. So I've got a bit of film and made a few notes about him.

When I do see Doull in action, he's tall and rangy with a decent action, a little reminiscent of Phil Newport of Worcestershire, but he has taken wickets in Test Matches. Word has it that he has more injuries than anybody we can ever think of.

They haven't got an out-and-out run-out fielder. They've got one or two donkeys in that department.

Of course, some of the New Zealand journalists gather round me and the inevitable question comes. 'What did you think of Zimbabwe?'

'I've got no comment. I've been in enough trouble already.'

There's a chance for some nice evenings out and in one harbourside restaurant, as I'm out with some of the television people, I'm just sorting out our table at the front desk when these two absolute stunners walk in. The most beautiful girls you've ever seen. Drop-dead gorgeous. And I'm just pushed to the back. It turns out that they're Miss World and Miss New Zealand and they were very very nice. Next day I hear on the radio that there's a photo opportunity if you want your picture taken with them. I don't make it. I'm not sure that it would be the thing for the snappers to see this fellow stood between Miss World and Miss New Zealand.

I'm certainly relaxed as we approach the First Test. We're all in good spirits from the results that we've had so far on the tour. If we're not right now, we never will be. I keep saying that we had the better of the Tests in Zimbabwe. We haven't started playing one-day matches. I might get a bit twitchy about those.

12

THE HOME SERVICE

PETER BAXTER
Thursday 23 January. In New Zealand Aggers will be having his breakfast on Friday morning, while I am setting off from home on a chilly Thursday evening to Broadcasting House in London and the 'Test Match Special' studio. It is all rather a far cry from the heat of Harare. I have had a sleep in the afternoon – that will become easier to do as the Test Match goes on – and I am turning round my days and nights over the next month, to feel the jet-lag without the benefit of the suntan.

For this series we are joining forces with Radio New Zealand for the commentary, renewing the old friendships of the cricket broadcasting fraternity. Bryan Waddle of Radio New Zealand has joined us in England for a couple of his country's tours and we last worked with him, sharing our commentary, in Pakistan and India during the 1996 World Cup. Both Aggers and I worked also with the former New Zealand captain, Jeremy Coney, in New Zealand five years ago. This sharing of commentary is a traditional friendly convenience, which is now, I think, unique to cricket and, rather sadly, becoming impractical with the differing demands of each other's broadcasts. The longest-standing of these relationships must be between the BBC and the Australian Broadcasting Corporation and yet, on England's last visit there, the demands of carrying commentary on

Radio Five Live meant that we had to mount a separate 'Test Match Special' operation, to the consternation of our Australian colleagues, who wondered if they had done something wrong.

During this series, 'Test Match Special' on Radio Four long wave will have some unavoidable interruptions and Radio New Zealand's Network One Sports will have frequent commercials. We will not hear those commercials, as our commentary comes direct from the ground, but the commentators will have the awkwardness of serving two masters. This is why I need to be in the studio, to smooth over the potentially awkward joints. This time I am not directly producing the commentary and so I have to fit in with a finished product from 14,000 miles away.

At least I should not on this occasion have the problem that confronted Radio New Zealand themselves some years ago, when they were taking commentary from Pakistan. They had contacted their counterparts there in advance and their commentator, Alan Richards, another old friend of 'Test Match Special', had been assured of a welcome in the Radio Pakistan commentary team. Duly he took over from the first Pakistani commentator. He did his twenty-minute spell and then handed on to the man he had been introduced to early in the day and whose name he had taken the precaution of writing down phonetically for just this moment. This new colleague thanked him warmly and then launched into twenty minutes' description of the game in Urdu. If Alan was surprised, you can imagine the shock in the studio in Wellington, where they were forced to switch to music until English commentary resumed – to be followed, no doubt, by an inquest into why no one had checked what language the Pakistanis were thinking of using.

These nights of 'Test Match Special' in Broadcasting House have their own memories. Of the 1974–75 tour of Australia, for instance, when David Lloyd was among those in the sights of Messrs Lillee and Thomson. Then we were

116

carrying commentary only on the last two hours of each day. Brian Johnston used to arrive at about four in the morning. 'Oh, Backers, I can't bear to hear it. What's the score? How is the old country doing?'

Then there was the night when we were taking commentary on a one-day international in Melbourne. I drove in to Broadcasting House in heavy rain, and for some reason we had been allocated a drama studio on the top floor. I sat in a curtained-off corner of this studio to introduce the programme, but the problems started before the programme did. First we seemed to have no lines to Australia. I tried to ring the commentary box at the MCG, but the studio phone was blocked to overseas calls. I rang the switchboard operator. 'My supervisor is the only person who can lift the block.'

'Let me speak to the supervisor, then.'

'She doesn't come in till six o'clock.'

'I will take personal responsibility to pay for the call myself if necessary.' Eventually I persuaded the operator to connect me.

We had to start the commentary on the telephone, with Christopher Martin-Jenkins handing over eventually to Neville Oliver. When he had been going for about ten minutes, another voice suddenly appeared on the air. We had a crossed line. 'And at the end of that over it's ...'

'Hello, who's that?'

'Now from the Southern end it's going to be ...'

'Hey, mate, who are you talking to?'

'The BBC.'

'You don't say! Hey, Jim, this joker's talking to the BBC ...'

By this time the BBC guidelines on crossed lines had convinced us that we could not risk hearing any more, and so I started commentating off the television pictures in the studio, while the studio managers wrestled with the communications. I talked on in the studio silence, until I became aware of a dripping sound beyond the curtains. The rain had started to penetrate the sixty-year-old slate roof of Broadcasting House. The studio managers were aware of this, too, and shortly – as I continued to describe the scene and the action from the television monitor – a man arrived with a bucket and disappeared behind the curtain.

Still I had to talk, as no sign of our line to Australia appeared and now I started to hear the bucket filling up. Drips were falling rapidly into an ever-growing pool and the sound was inescapable. Hysteria at the whole situation was on the verge of taking over when the welcome words came in my headphones, 'You can hand over to Melbourne now.'

I hope tonight's broadcast will be more sophisticated. The first priority is a call to Aggers. 'What's the weather like?' Check on the commentary team, then eventually the toss and the teams. At last it's 'Let's join Bryan Waddle, who's already talking to listeners in New Zealand ...'

13

AUCKLAND: DUCK SOUP

DAVID LLOYD

The story of Dominic Cork's injury has been building up while I have been watching the New Zealand practice match in Auckland. I have thought to myself, if there's any real problem somebody will contact me. So I've just been sitting and watching the game.

When the team arrive in Auckland after the win in Hamilton, the physiotherapist, Wayne Morton, comes to see me straight away and tells me about the injury and the treatment. Cork needs a couple of days' rest and then he'll have to bowl on Thursday, the day before the Test, when he'll have to prove he's right. If he's not right on Thursday afternoon, he isn't right on Friday morning.

So all the attention is focused on Dominic Cork while we get on with our business. I don't even ask Dominic 'How are you?' because I've got other people to do that. I've got medical people and they will tell me. I've got enough players apart from him. But after his first spell I do go to him and ask, 'How do you feel?'

'I'm getting there. I'll be all right.'

I tell him, 'You'll come in and have another bowl and a bat after a rest. So let me know again.' That all turns out favourably. Now we'll leave it to the very last minute tomorrow morning. He will be playing, but if he has a reaction overnight obviously we'll look at it again. But we

119

know then that he will play.

Dominic has had a very difficult winter with his much-publicised personal problems. His work since he's come out here has been adequate. I wouldn't expect him to race through teams – although he has the ability to do it – because he's had a winter at home. We have watched him very closely when he joined the team and he looked fit enough. He's taken wickets in the two matches where there's been some help. I believe he's a lad who thrives on you putting an arm round him to encourage him. There are others who you can keep kicking up the backside. Darren Gough, for instance, is totally different. He's just an uncomplicated character who goes like a bull at a gate.

There's a piece Christopher Martin-Jenkins wrote that I carry around and every now and again I remind them of some of the things in it. What we're looking for is flair and imagination in batting; orthodox batting; strong batting; a tough, ruthless team with an emphasis on the physical and psychological; superlative fielding. I have shown this to Darren. 'Just to remind you, that's what we're after.'

He's reading through it. 'What does that mean, superlative?'

'It means we want some aggression. Out in the field we're at 'em all the time. You don't want to give them any respite. You're in there with superlative fielding. You're diving at the ball and attacking the ball. The same with bowling. You want to be at 'em and aggressive.'

His response to that is, 'Well, why don't you just tell us to go out and knock their heads off? Why don't you use words we understand?' So they're totally different characters in that respect.

JONATHAN AGNEW
The injury to Cork dominates our previews to the First Test. Two days before the match, and only three days after he has hobbled off the ground at Hamilton, he is spotted running and even sprinting with Wayne Morton, and next day he is

able to bowl in the nets. It quickly becomes clear that he will be able to take his place, after all, and at least the media's interest in his condition has diverted attention away from the struggling form of Mike Atherton.

The pitch looks green and rather damp. As is the case at most of New Zealand's cricket venues, Eden Park is primarily a rugby ground, which means that the wicket area – or 'block', as it is called in this part of the world – has to be extensively repaired and often relaid at the end of every rugby season. This means that it is very difficult to know how each pitch will behave, particularly over five days.

DL

It's becoming an old story on this tour, but both in Zimbabwe and now here we've had horrific weather. There's been lots and lots of rain throughout the tour and when you talk to groundsmen they all sing the same song. 'I'm a little bit behind in my preparations. I've not had the sunshine to dry the top off the pitch.' And you can tell quite clearly that the pitches are damp. They've been wet three or four days before the match. The groundsmen then roll it and get it flat and then want sunshine to dry it off, and it's not happened really anywhere we've been. Now Auckland is a classic case.

I am going to the ground daily to watch the pitch develop for the Test Match. The groundsman wets the pitch and then he wets it again. He says, 'I'm set fair for good weather. It's going to twenty-four or twenty-five degrees. It'll burn the top off.' The pitch is covered, because it rains, and he is behind. There's grass around. He tells us that it normally cracks and that grass burns off. 'This pitch, when the game starts, will be brown.'

Well, it isn't. It is green and damp.

We're keen generally to play two spinners. We played two last August at The Oval with Robert Croft on his debut alongside Ian Salisbury, and we played both spinners in the two Tests in Zimbabwe. We like the balance of playing two

121

spinners and we've come into this Test with that same view.

Now, though, everything tells us that we've got to play the extra seamer and just have one spinner. The other thing is the strange shape of the ground, because Eden Park is a rugby ground with the pitch set at an angle, so that for a right-handed batter the boundary at square leg is fifty yards, if that. Everything tells us to play one spinner and the New Zealanders see it exactly the same way.

So we opt for the all-rounder, Craig White, and Alan Mullally as well. I think we've been very fair with Alan. We've got to look for consistency in selection and I think we've given him a good run. The spin bowler we opt for is Phil Tufnell over Robert Croft, partly because of that short square leg boundary and a gut feeling, which I'm all for. If there's going to be a choice, what's the gut feeling? And the gut feeling is Tufnell. On this occasion it's Tufnell. And then you've got to speak to Robert and say, 'Look, you're not dropped, whatever anybody says. This is a tactical selection.' He's disappointed, but takes it well, as he should do. But sometimes people don't. He rallies round the team and gets involved with everything on the periphery, which you've got to do in support of the team, even though you're not playing, and I know he is hurting inside. He does that aspect of his job as a tourist brilliantly.

JA

England win the toss and it is no surprise to learn that, in what appear to be extremely helpful bowling conditions, Atherton has invited New Zealand to bat first. However, after only seventeen overs, all five of England's bowlers, including Phil Tufnell, have been in action. Cork, Mullally, Gough and White have squandered the new ball, and although there is exaggerated movement both in the air and off the seam, none of them has bowled straight enough to worry Pocock and Young, the New Zealand opening batsmen. It has been a terrible waste and by lunch New Zealand are 72 without loss.

A traditional Maori welcome for Dominic Cork. England were also glad to welcome him after he had missed the Zimbabwe leg of the tour. (*Allsport*)

New Zealand brought in Emily Drumm for an informal game.
Mike Atherton, watching her bowl, was diplomatic when she later
caught him. (*Allsport*)

England v New Zealand Academy. Jack Russell runs out Mark Greatbatch.
(*Allsport*)

Mike Atherton, checking his technique with a video camera, and a fishing rod. (*Allsport*)

Off duty: David Lloyd at the helm. (*Allsport*)

Auckland, the First Test. *Above:* Dipak Patel trapped lbw first ball to Darren Gough. *Below left:* Graham Thorpe, in form at last, on his way to a century; *below right:* Craig White shows his disappointment as New Zealand save the match. (*Allsport*)

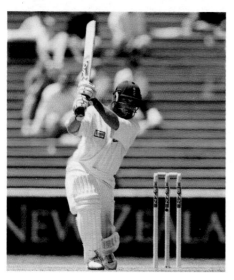

Daniel Vettori, New Zealand's young spinner, troubled England batsmen in the
Second Test at Wellington. (*Allsport*)

The Second Test. *Above:* Stephen Fleming is caught and bowled by Andrew Caddick. *Below:* Mike Atherton and Darren Gough celebrate England's victory. (*Allsport*)

England win the Third Test at Christchurch, and the series.

Left: Robert Croft who took seven wickets in the match, with Darren Gough.
Below: The victorious team.
(*Allsport*)

Mike Atherton and Lee Germon, after the one-day series is shared. (*Allsport*)

DL

The captain later says he's not seen anything like it. By the bowlers' own admission their performance is horrific and by the fourteenth over Tufnell is on, trying to get some semblance of stability into our attack. We have another bad session, which is something I've been striving to get rid of. We say, in any public statements we make, that we're moving forward, we're progressing, but we must get rid of this habit of the poor spell. We had one on the first day in Bulawayo, when we let them get away to make 376, and then we had a poor batting spell in Harare, when we were all out for 156. Now we've done it again on this first morning in Auckland, when you really want to stamp your authority on the game. In Ian Chappell's words, 'You poke the opposition in the chest from ball one.' Well, we're not poking anybody on this morning. It has been a dreadful performance.

They are 72 for no wicket at lunch, they've used all five bowlers, and I don't go anywhere near them. I just sit on my own and leave them to it. That is a conscious decision on my part. They will know exactly what I think by my not going to the dressing room, just keeping out of the way.

We haven't put them in expecting to have them 69 all out in a session, as we did at Hamilton. That only happens once or twice in a career. We just think it's going to do something. The pitch is behind in preparation and the groundsman has said that there's every likelihood that the best time to bowl will be in these first two sessions, and then it will flatten out into a decent sort of pitch and get slower and slower as the game progresses. He's very open about it, so it's just a common-sense decision that we bowl first. It may be that bowling first means 280 or 290 all out. Good effort. Well done. It's a five-day game. In a four-day county game, you'd think if they got 350 you'd still be in it.

JA

At last, in the thirty-fourth over, Mullally has Young trapped lbw for 44 and Adam Parore has quickly edged Cork down the leg side to Alec Stewart. Stephen Fleming, the tall, elegant left-hander, is now at the crease and, unperturbed by the loss of Nathan Astle to White for 10 and Justin Vaughan to Cork for 3 – which leaves New Zealand on 215 for five – he and Chris Cairns, who is dropped on 5, see their team through to 233 for five at the close of play on the first day. There is an overwhelming feeling amongst the English media that New Zealand have been allowed to get away.

DL

That first session this morning has been another that has had to be dragged back and, to their credit, they have dragged it back. The three wickets after tea have done that, but putting down Chris Cairns just before the close has been a big blow. That would have been 220 for 6 and we'd really have been on top.

JA

Despite their efforts with the ball on the first morning England are still very much in the match, but they need to take early wickets on the second morning. However, the shaggy-haired Cairns and Fleming have other ideas and it is not until ten minutes before lunch that they finally remove Cairns, caught behind off White for 67 after he and Fleming have put on 118 for the sixth wicket. Lee Germon, New Zealand's captain, threatens to dig in with Fleming, but Gough dismisses him, caught behind for 14, and poor Dipak Patel, who I remember so well from his days at Worcestershire, is lbw to Gough's next ball. Meanwhile Fleming's century comes from 198 balls and includes one 6 and fifteen 4s. A little boy dressed in shorts and proudly brandishing a New Zealand flag dashes on to the field and shakes him by the hand, but Fleming is rapidly running out of partners. Simon Doull edges Gough to Knight at second slip to allow the number 11, Danny Morrison, to make his grand entrance to an unusual chorus of loud quacks from the hundreds of duck-callers he has sold on the ground in aid of his testimonial. No one has ever been dismissed more times for nought in Test cricket than Morrison, but he has reached the dizzy heights of six when Fleming is finally the last man out, caught and bowled by Cork, for a memorable 129. New Zealand are all out for 390, with Gough taking 4 for 91 and Cork 3 for 96.

DL

So, despite only getting one wicket in the morning session, an hour after lunch we've knocked them over. In the context of it all, 320 would have been all right and 390 doesn't mean we're out of it, because, as the groundsman has said, it'll flatten out. And it does. It's not bad at all.

Atherton is the same as ever. He plays a good Test Match innings at a decent Test Match tempo for an opening batsman. He's never any different. Works hard, gets on with it, greedy for runs. He gets frustrated, maybe, when he doesn't score, but he gets on with the job of captaining the side and looking after the players.

JA

England have desperately needed a good start and, although Knight is quickly lbw to the medium-pacer, Simon Doull, Atherton, typically, has shrugged off worries about his form to see England through to 123 for 1 at the close of the second day. The beginning of his innings was scratchy, but I was behind the microphone when he forced a cover boundary off the back foot and, immediately, I recognised it as being a sign that he was back to his best. Indeed, a smile behind the grille of his helmet suggested that Atherton knew it, too. He falls after lunch on the third day in the unluckiest of ways, caught and bowled off Patel, the off-spinner, but only because a firm on-drive has rebounded off Vaughan, who is fielding at short mid-on. England are 200 for 2, still 190 runs behind, and this becomes 222 for 3 when Patel winkles out Hussain for 8.

Meanwhile, at the other end, Stewart is flourishing. Somehow, despite the fact that he has kept wicket throughout New Zealand's innings and only had eight overs to wait before he walked out at number three, he summons the energy to play an unforgettable innings. It is Stewart at his very best: his timing is immaculate, particularly off his legs, and he regularly peppers the cover boundary with sumptuous front-foot drives. He scores 173, the highest ever score by an England wicket-keeper, before getting a leading edge and knocking back a return catch to Doull. When he begins his innings, England are 372 behind New Zealand and in a potentially awkward position. When he strides off the field, having struck 23 fours and one six, the difference between the two teams is only 86.

DL

Now we're moving in on this 390. We've a strong batting line-up. Stewart has continued to play well and he and Athers have carried on into the third day. Alec's still happy keeping wicket and batting at three and he's playing well. He's made a big hundred, but his Surrey colleague, Graham Thorpe, has this question mark. When is he going to convert fifties into hundreds? This time he does. His mix-up with Crawley, which ends in a run-out, puts a bit of a damper on it, because we would have been absolutely cruising without that. It's as good a shot as is played in the Test Match. Crawley hits a straight-bat back-foot shot through straight mid-on. Doull dives left, scrambles the ball, Crawley's damn near run two and he's out through a misunderstanding. It's a poor piece of cricket, but it doesn't seem to affect their friendship.

JA

It has been a shocking run-out and entirely Graham Thorpe's fault. Initially, Thorpe responds to Crawley's call, but inexplicably he changes his mind and dashes back to his crease. Crawley, having run the entire length of the pitch,

126

has no option but to try to get back to the other end. It's too late and Doull's throw to Germon is deadly accurate. It was Crawley's call and he had every right to expect Thorpe to run. From the sidelines it looks absolutely dreadful – and, worse still, White is immediately lbw to Vaughan's first ball. Suddenly, England are 339 for 6, still 51 runs adrift.

DL

Craig White is slightly disappointed to be given out, as he's a lad trying to establish himself in the side. But we've put it to Cork that we need some runs from the lower order and he gets stuck in and makes 59. Cork has to play more innings like that, and he can. I've seen him open the innings for Derbyshire and play well in a controlled way, not a harum-scarum fashion.

People are saying we're going slow, but we are manoeuvring a position. We need a substantial lead to bowl at. It's important to get your runs in the first innings. Sometimes with defensive fields you've just got to sit in, and we do. We've got two guys with hundreds and we've got Cork at number eight, who gets nearly 60, and we pass 500. So it's a classic case. They've got 390, we manoeuvre past them. Who's winning this game now? That puts a tremendous amount of pressure on the team that now has to come in 131 runs behind, realistically doing nothing more than trying to save the game.

JA

After the Crawley debacle, Thorpe has owed England a big innings. He has certainly been as frustrated as everyone else by his failure to turn fifties into big scores and has needed no reminding that since his first Test century, on his debut against Australia in 1993, he has made only one more. However, he has passed 50 on no fewer than eighteen occasions. This time, there is no mistake. Thorpe scores 119 in five and a half hours, an innings which puts England into the lead, and it only ends when he slips as he plays a

127

delivery from Cairns and hits his own wicket.

Cork's knock of 59 is outstanding and promises so much for the future. He batted for four hours with barely a sign of the impetuosity which tends to lead to his downfall. There is no reason why Cork should not bat at number 6, and this innings is proof of that.

Even Tufnell and Mullally get in on the act, adding 43 for the last wicket, and, for a change, England's lower order has batted responsibly. England's lead is 131.

Young is quickly caught by Hussain in the gully off Cork for 3, Gough traps Pocock lbw for 20 and when Tufnell takes the crucial wicket of Fleming just before the close, New Zealand are 47 for 3 and in desperate trouble. There is a full day's play remaining, the pitch is taking spin and they are still 84 runs behind.

DL

At the end of the fourth day we've got them 56 for 3 and they're three good wickets – Young, Pocock and Fleming. They're still 75 behind. Now there is only one team winning this. It will take them the next session of play to get level with us, and we're congratulating ourselves and asking how many wickets we can take in the first session tomorrow. So we're focused on moving in for the win. I'm fully confident that we will win. The press don't seem to have confidence in us, but they're all like that. England don't win so many nowadays.

JA

Naturally, there is tremendous excitement in and around the England camp at the start of the final day. Contrary to popular belief, the English media desperately wants England to win, and this would be their first overseas victory for two years. I believe that Tufnell will be the key bowler because, with bowlers' rough on both sides of the pitch, he should pose the batsmen plenty of problems, particularly if fielders are brought in to close catching positions. However, as a

128

cautionary note, the final paragraph of my preview for BBC Radio that morning reads as follows: 'I fancy, though, that England's biggest obstacle today will be themselves. Test victories rarely fall into your lap, and have the bowlers who performed so inadequately earlier in the match got the self-belief to beat a team which is equally low in confidence?'

I am not in any way trying to be clever by repeating those sentences in the light of what does occur on this extraordinary final day. I am merely illustrating the reservations I have about England at the time. Far too often in recent years, England have sat back and waited for something to happen rather than seizing the initiative themselves. After all that has happened earlier on this tour, and particularly in Bulawayo, I doubt that England have either the confidence or the inspiration to win the game. Cynical, perhaps, but honest.

Even so, the first forty-five minutes of play this morning are astonishing. Germon and Parore bat absolutely calmly and without the least pressure. There is a fielder on the third-man fence. The quick bowlers are given only two slips and a gully. Thirty-two runs are added, and without Parore eventually running Germon out it is debatable if England would have captured a single wicket.

However, Hussain's throw from cover point hits the stumps direct, and in the next over Parore, who is no doubt wracked with guilt, has a brainstorm. He charges Tufnell and is comfortably stumped by Stewart for 13. The floodgates open. New Zealand lose five wickets for 49 runs before lunch to Tufnell and Mullally, so at the interval they are still 26 behind with only two wickets left. Bryan Waddle, one of my colleagues in the commentary box, is left to sum up the morning session. 'The wheels have come off here at Eden Park,' he announces. 'Not just one; the whole lot of them! Back to the studio.'

DL

We have had a great morning session. Somehow we have

129

got that spark of magic. The great moment that has started it has been when Parore ran out his captain. He has taken a run to one of the best fielders in world cricket, Hussain, coming on to the ball, and he has thrown the stumps down. Not content with that, Parore has got himself out stumped, coming down the pitch to a ball from Philip Tufnell that has bitten and turned. So after forty minutes when nothing has happened we've got that little bit of magic and we get on a roll. We've just got right into them and it's a great moment when Dipak Patel bags a pair with the last ball before lunch, lbw to Mullally, because he's a lad who can stick around. They're 105 for 8 and they're still 26 behind. We're cock-a-hoop, but the word is, 'Stay calm. We've not finished yet; we've got some work to do.' I hear later from Nathan Astle that they are all packing their bags in the interval. 'That's it. We're out of it. The game's over. We've lost.' Astle tells me they're just going through the token gestures of saying, 'You support me and I'll stay there.'

JA

The talk in the press box is of afternoon rounds of golf and early departures for Wanganui, the venue for the following four-day match. Astle, who scored a century against England in the World Cup a year before, is still at the crease, and although he and Doull put on 37 for the ninth wicket before Doull is yorked by a Gough in-swinger for 26, the result does not look in doubt. It is not a question of whether England will win; simply a matter of when.

Another round of duck-calls greets Morrison. New Zealand's lead is now 11 and even the most optimistic Kiwi does not imagine that it can possibly stretch much beyond that.

DL

Danny the Duck. He's not fooling anybody. We've talked about Danny Morrison on this tour. When he came in to bat at Palmerston North, he came in with a girlie magazine stuck down his front pad. Everybody has a laugh and a joke, and so we tell the players, 'Don't get involved with him.' He's like Ray East of Essex. He wants to be everybody's mate out there and to talk to everybody. 'Shut him out. We don't speak to the guy.' Because Ray East could bat. He'd give everybody the impression that he couldn't bat, but he could.

JA
The partnership between Astle and Doull has clearly had an effect on England's morale and, from the distance of the commentary box, there appears to be an alarming lack of animation in the middle. The quick bowlers completely lose their way when Morrison is facing, peppering him with short stuff and then trying to bowl the perfect yorker rather than simply treating him like any other batsman. Meanwhile Tufnell bowls too flat. I remember Ray Illingworth saying that a spinner should toss the ball up above a tail-ender's eye-line in order to make him misjudge the length, but the more frustrated Tufnell becomes the more he pushes the ball through.

Worse, though, is the lack of any ideas or inspiration from the captain. England will argue that they tried everything, but the fact is that they do not. They do not even try to attack until it is too late, and neither do they attempt anything different or unusual. Why does Atherton himself not toss up a few leg spinners? He might have a bad back, but he is able to throw himself about in the field and bat for four and a half hours with no ill effects, and all he has to do is turn his arm over. And what about Crawley, Thorpe, Hussain – anybody? And why is Morrison not crowded with close fielders, especially when Tufnell is bowling at him? It is obvious that he has no intention of hitting out, but he is not put under anything like enough pressure.

DL
I think Danny would still have been batting weeks later. We hit him on the head twice with balls that he seemed to be

happy to nod back to the bowler. Now we are not getting that bit of magic. We feel that with New Zealand you don't have to crowd them out with close fielders. They get themselves out. Stop their flow of runs and they'll do something quite bizarre. In the morning it has worked perfectly when we nicked five out. That was exactly the way Zimbabwe got us out. They didn't crowd us out with four slips. They had a third man, one on the drive, one at mid-wicket and another at fine leg. We have decided that that is a good strategy. We will look to get them out in legitimate areas, but we'll just push back and defend – what we call 'an in-out field'. There are fielders saving fours, but we've got catchers as well. It's worked perfectly in the morning.

When Danny Morrison comes in, knowing him from his time at Lancashire and the matches that we've played against him, we have a long on, a deep mid-wicket and a couple of catchers round the bat. He'll hole out. But he's no intention of holing out. So when that doesn't work, we bring everybody in and crowd him. We bowl over the wicket, we bowl round the wicket, we've fast bowlers bowling off-spinners or putting a little leg-spinner in. He could still be in in a week. People afterwards come up to me and say, 'Why didn't the captain bowl?' He just doesn't. He has a bad back. He's going to have to go out with a notice, 'I HAVE A BAD BACK. I CAN'T BOWL.' 'Why didn't Graham Thorpe bowl?' He wasn't fancied. Somebody asks, 'Why didn't they put the wicket-keeper on?' My answer is, 'Just get back in your bed.' Morrison is playing with the best dead bat you'll ever see.

I can feel it drifting away in the mid-afternoon. You're looking round thinking, 'Where's this spark going to come from?' Darren Gough is spent. He's tried a couple of bouncers that haven't gone anywhere. That's when you feel that there's nothing there. It's not spinning and it's only bouncing shin-high. There's nothing that's going to rear up and take him on the glove or frighten him. We just don't get that spark.

132

JA

After a while, smiles begin to reappear on the faces of the New Zealand journalists and calculators begin to appear. Valuable overs are being lost now, and New Zealand's lead is building dangerously. Memories of Bulawayo come flooding back as we begin to realise that a frantic run chase will be required if England are to take the last wicket and go for victory. At the start of the last fifteen overs New Zealand are 104 ahead, which, when the two overs between innings are taken away, means that England have to score at a rate of eight runs per over, even if they manage to get Morrison or Astle out immediately. A worried-looking John Barclay appears at the commentary box door. He wants to check out the situation regarding the number of overs in the last hour. David Lloyd, who has been sitting beneath our window for much of the afternoon, has now disappeared.

Morrison is a brave tail-end batsman and this is his innings of a lifetime. He does not offer a single chance and he bats for a total of two and three-quarter hours and survives 133 balls for his 14 not out. Astle has been superb. He has continued to play his strokes regardless of New Zealand's parlous position and when, finally, he advances to Craig White and thumps him through extra cover for four, not only does he reach his third century in the most emphatic fashion, but he also moves Atherton to concede that victory is now beyond him. As the batsmen run off, jubilantly hugging each other, Gough strides up to Astle and hands him a stump as a souvenir. It is a touching gesture.

DL

We should have won the game. Of course we should. Everyone is pointing to us and saying, 'You should have won.' We haven't, though we were the ones who were winning. But the atmosphere afterwards suggests that they're the side who've won. They've had their backs to the wall almost throughout the game, yet they're the ones who have got the accolades. I suppose it was inevitable when

133

they've saved a game from that position, but we know we are better than them.

Immediately afterwards I have to do a TV interview with Nathan Astle, who has finished the match with the four that took him to his hundred. I congratulate him and say, 'That was a terrific effort from you and your mate. It was wonderful to see, but not good if you were in our camp.'

The interviewer asks him, 'What were the England team like?' He says, 'They never stopped coming at us. There was a bit of chirp round the bat, as there would be, a bit of banter. They tried all sorts of things, but they'd never have got us out. We knew they weren't going to get us out, but they kept coming.'

In the dressing room afterwards there are a few tears, a few things kicked around and a bit of self-expression. Then quiet – very, very quiet. We're working then – with John Emburey, the manager and the captain – because there'll be some that'll be worse than others. One of them says, 'This is such a cruel game at times.' Nothing has been said and he's just come out with that.

I sit with him and say, 'You're dead right, it is. You've got to savour your good times. And we'll have some good times.' And it takes a long while for anybody to come round. Then I'm looking round and thinking, 'Oh Lord, we've got another game in a day's time.'

14

A WOBBLE IN WANGANUI

JONATHAN AGNEW
One of the most enjoyable aspects of touring is having the opportunity to visit new places. Because the venues of the Test Matches tend to be fixed in every country, the only chance we have to travel off the beaten track is between the main games and, following their exhausting final day at Auckland, England set off for Wanganui, which lies on the south-west coast of New Zealand's North island.

The team fly to Palmerston North and complete the journey with an hour's drive in a bus. I prefer to fly to Wellington, the capital, and pick up a hire car. My trip from there to Wanganui takes a little over two hours.

Wanganui is known as the River City (all the towns in this part of the world seem to have alternative names; Palmerston North, for example, is the Friendly City and Christchurch is the Garden City). It is a pretty little town, set a mile or two inland, and through which flows the Whanganui River.

As I pull up outside the splendidly named Grand Hotel, which is an old turn-of-the-century hostelry, I am slightly put off by the large wooden notice which creakily sways in the breeze over the front door. 'PUB BEDS AVAILABLE: ONLY $20', it reads. Hotel rooms are critical to morale on tour; they are, after all, your home for the length of your stay and I am more than just a little perturbed when, having

135

battled my way through one of the three downstairs bars, I open the door to room 204. I need not have worried. The receptionist, who is clearly delighted to have a group of English tourists in her hotel, shows me round personally and assures me that it is even possible to telephone England from the room. Reassuring news for a broadcaster.

Given that revelation, and bearing in mind that Peter Baxter has optimistically ordered a high-quality digital circuit at the ground, I decide that an early inspection of Victoria Park is in order. High on a hill and overlooking the sea on the right-hand side, it turns out to be a splendid and very large, open cricket field. Better still, a man from Telecom has just completed the installation of my line, which he has placed in a comfortable caravan at long off. My colleagues in the written media are to be housed in a large marquee at extra cover. The pitch looks rather rough and, as I survey the rural surroundings, I wonder what the England team will make of it all because it is a complete contrast to the modern, built-up stadium in Auckland. Hopefully, I think, they will enjoy the break and make the most of the relaxed atmosphere.

DAVID LLOYD

If we'd won in Auckland there'd be a different subconscious attitude to the match we've now got to play against New Zealand 'A' in Wanganui, because we know that we have got to play the five lads who missed the Auckland Test Match in order to prepare for the next Test Match. The fixture has been agreed between the boards, so we just have to get on with it, but I am saying, 'This is a difficult fixture in view of what's gone on.' We'd have a different perception of this game now if we'd won the Test Match. It would be a more enjoyable game. As it is, we were the ones who were thwarted and we are so disappointed.

Wanganui is lovely. The ground is a park. Nothing more than a park. One of our travelling groups of supporters has rung the ground saying, 'Would you reserve us twenty-five

136

seats in your best stand.'

The man in charge is delighted by this. 'We don't have a stand.'

'Well, can you save us twenty-five seats.'

He says, 'We haven't got seats. Everybody brings their own.'

I have to say to our players, 'This is the fixture. We're playing it and I want a performance from you. I don't want any of that lot coming up to me and saying, "They weren't ready for it. They weren't focused." You put a professional performance on.' I think they are focused as well as can be expected.

JA

In the morning, New Zealand 'A' win the toss and decide to bat first. England bring in all five players who did not feature in the First Test: Ronnie Irani, Jack Russell, Robert Croft, Andy Caddick and Chris Silverwood. By late afternoon the New Zealand youngsters have been bowled out for 181, with Silverwood taking a career-best 6 for 44.

He bowls with great enthusiasm and swings the ball away from the bat. And although Matthew Horne scores 64, the most notable resistance comes, again, from the last-wicket pair of Geoff Allott and Jason Mills, who hang around, Morrison-style, for fifty minutes. All things considered, it is an excellent effort by England, who appear to have shrugged off their disappointment remarkably quickly.

DL

Chris Silverwood bowls well, gets the ball in the right places and takes six wickets, but seems tired and that is a slight worry to us. He's a young lad and has all the fitness in the world. He's had one full season and he runs a hell of a long way and takes a lot out of himself in the delivery. Here it's hot and dry.

I describe it as 'a dirty pitch' and that gets misconstrued. There's a lot of debris all over the ground from the trees and you're coughing and spluttering. It's dusty. It's not mani-cured. It's nice with the view – the sea's in the background and the trees – there are nice people. I'm asked at a press conference, 'What do you think of Wanganui?'

'Wanganui's very nice. This ground's lovely and very pretty – albeit a park ground. The people have been great and so accommodating to us. The ladies who've made the lunches have been terrific.'

That gets interpreted in the press as, 'England coach says, "Lunches great. Let's push off." ' Which is not exactly what has been said.

JA

The gloss is knocked off the day by the loss of three wickets before the close. Two of them, Knight and Crawley, fall to the left-armer, Allott, who charges in like a man possessed. He knows that a recall to the New Zealand team beckons and, sometimes achieving startling bounce, he spectacularly grabs his chance. Heath Davis nips out Atherton, who gloves an attempted hook to the wicket-keeper for five. England reach 30 for 3 at the close, still 151 runs behind.

DL

The pitch is really crusty. They've brought this lad Geoff Allott in, who has the pace to knock the top off the pitch. Nobody else has the pace to knock the top off. None of our lads has his pace and their other bowlers didn't have that pace. But Allott is a handful, because he bowls fast. He doesn't care, perhaps, where he runs on the pitch.

JA

The next morning is a shambles as England lose their remaining 7 wickets for only 77 runs. Allott and Davis run through the middle order who, having seen a delivery from Davis to Hussain explode off a length, do not seem to relish the opportunity to bat with any great determination. Irani plays a spirited innings of 40 from only 68 balls but a glance through the scorecard shows that only Hussain, with 14, Knight, 11, and Silverwood, who also made 11, reach double figures. As they take the field, 74 runs behind, England look dispirited and make little secret of the fact that they would prefer to have been somewhere – apparently anywhere – else.

Silverwood is not able to repeat his heroics of the first innings. Although England hope to find the same unreliable bounce which had caused them so many problems when they batted, their bowlers are at least a yard slower than the New Zealanders and, consequently, hit the pitch nowhere near as hard. Craig Spearman scores 47, Chris Harris (another Test hopeful) 71, and Lorne Howell 66 as New Zealand 'A' are eventually dismissed for 288, setting England a highly unlikely 363 to win. Silverwood concedes 74 runs from 17 wicketless overs, but at least Caddick takes the chance to find some semblance of rhythm to take 3 for 52.

This game provides our first glimpse of umpire Brent 'Billy' Bowden. We've seen him on television officiating in the domestic one-day matches. He is thoroughly eccentric and is clearly trying to make a name for himself; much as, I suppose, Dickie Bird had done twenty years ago. Billy is a thin, wiry chap with long, straggly hair and specialises in alternative umpiring signals. These are loosely based on the traditional means of signalling fours, byes, wides and so on but have been gloriously embellished with hip gyrations and sensual rubs of the thigh to the extent that umpire Bowden would not look out of place performing in a strip joint in downtown Bangkok. His leg bye signal is particularly sexy: I describe it on Radio New Zealand as looking like a young lady seductively peeling off her right stocking. Billy hears about this and, rather earnestly, comes over to thank me after play finishes on the third day.

By this stage, England are facing certain defeat which, to be honest, has been the case since they were bowled out so cheaply on the second day. Within five minutes of the lunch break on the fourth, it is all over with England becoming the first touring team to lose a first-class match in New Zealand for fourteen years. Jack Russell does his best, scoring 61 from 82 balls while tugging at his shirt and shouting 'Remember the three lions!' to his batting partners. But apart from Croft, who scores a gutsy 49, the rest of the lower order subsides and Tufnell's pitiful slog to long-off to finish the game said it all. Within forty minutes the team bus screeches to a halt outside the pavilion steps and the England team is on its way to Wellington.

However, there has been just enough time for David Lloyd's press conference, which provides so much copy for my colleagues in the written media. Perhaps it is simply Bumble's way to be sarcastic when he is under pressure – I am convinced that some of the press do not understand his Northern sense of humour – but I am also not sure that he really meant to say that he was 'pleased and proud' of the way England played this match. That is the quote which Paul Weaver enjoys most of all. Writing in the *Guardian*, he speculates whether or not the men in white coats, who were in close attendance, were necessarily umpires! It is a very amusing line but the result is that relations between the players and the press sink still further.

DL

We've been playing an 'A' team, who are all wanting to get into the New Zealand Test side. They're like fireflies, all over you. It has been a difficult game for us after what has gone on in Auckland. We've travelled here the day after by plane and bus. Someone writes in the local paper that the coach calls it an arduous journey. I haven't said that at all. I have said it would be a difficult game. I wish they would get their facts right. Still, it's a good story for the press, England's reaction to the disappointment of Auckland. I am planning the next Test Match. I say to the press, 'This has no bearing on the Wellington Test Match.' Two of them think I need a straitjacket.

Someone describes me as Basil Fawlty, but that's a bit of fun. After all, he was part of one of the most successful programmes ever made on television. I get calls from mates at home, 'Who's that chap who's writing this or that about you?'

I say, 'He's all right. Good lad. I've been out to dinner with him. Played golf.'

'You must be joking.'

I say, 'That's how it is. They're doing their job. I'm doing mine. I don't read 'em, so I get on with it.'

I'm not sure all the press understand my humour. That's been said to me by a couple of my bosses. I am annoyed that we've lost and I want to get to Wellington. The press are having their lunch. I breeze in and say, 'All right, you lot. If you want anything from me, let's be having you. I've got a proper game to go to.' I feel that I've been a bit victimised and I'll give them something to get stirred up about. And it does. The lead is throwing sparks off the paper. I get a bit mischievous and say, when they ask what we're doing when we get to Wellington, 'We'll have a rest. We'll have the rest we didn't get after the Auckland Test.' I quite enjoy that little bit of banter with them.

One journalist, whose name I won't divulge, has said to me, 'You're handling it really well. And I know that you understand that whatever you say, you're meat to the lions if you lose.'

But we'll see who wins in Wellington.

15

WINNING WAYS IN WELLINGTON

JONATHAN AGNEW
I really believe that the fate of this entire tour – and, with it, Mike Atherton's future as captain – depends on what happens over the next five days. New Zealand have their problems in that Chris Cairns has sprained an ankle and is clearly less than fully fit, but even though England should have comprehensively won the First Test, they now find themselves under intense scrutiny.

I did not go to Zimbabwe, but I reckon that there have been eight low points on this tour up to now, and every one would have had its own deflating effect on the morale of the players: the loss to the President's XI in Harare, the defeat by Mashonaland, the dramatic Bulawayo Test, each of the defeats in the three one-day internationals in Zimbabwe, the Auckland final day and the debacle at Wanganui. Having just watched that particular game, I am very concerned about the mood in the camp. Either that, or England's players have perfected the art of looking sullen and miserable. I accept that the pitch was not great and it was not a Test match, but it is shortsighted, I think, to say that the result did not matter because it is from that level that England have to start today as they look for only their third away victory since we were all here, at the Basin Reserve, five years ago.

During the pre-Test press conference I ask Atherton how he feels about the captaincy issue, and although his reply is

142

along the lines of not caring if his job is on the line over the next fortnight, I think what he really means to say is that he is not going to allow it to distract him.

DAVID LLOYD

We've had lots of bad weather around, and again we've been into the business of there being no available practice, so we've just had running around and fielding and doing what we could. We've been gathering information about the pitch from people like Paul Allott, who played here for a couple of seasons, and Bob Carter, who used to be at Northampton and is now the coach here. It looks dry. We hear that there'll be pace in it. There'll be good bounce and carry. The groundsman says, 'It'll be cupped hands for the wicket-keeper.' So your wicket-keeper will be taking the ball from the quicker bowlers round his chest.

Meanwhile we're enjoying Wellington, with all the yachts from the round-the-world race in the harbour, about to sail the next leg, across to Sydney. We've been invited down to have a look at the boats and maybe have a sail. We don't actually do that, but we meet a number of crews and it's fascinating to hear how those crews are selected. Chay Blyth's there, talking to Lord MacLaurin, and it's all very relaxing.

It's good, too, to have a lot of English spectators here. They really do give us a lift. You've got the Barmy Army element, who do come in for some criticism, but the fact is that they do have a structured leadership in Charlie and Alison from Brixton, who are both police sergeants, I believe. They orchestrate everything and they're also doing a charity collection and selling shirts for the children's cancer effort in New Zealand. So they're round the grounds, selling the T-shirts and so on, and they raise thousands of dollars, which tends to go unnoticed. We get some letters saying, 'My day was ruined by the chanting and singing of the mindless morons.' Well, they're not actually like that. There's a good soul to them.

143

The other, more regular, touring groups of England supporters far outnumber opposition spectators. The locals tell us so and they're disappointed that they haven't got more of their own people at the matches. It does make a difference to us.

There's a real determination in our side. I know that we've come under the fire of criticism from the game in Wanganui, but I'm protecting the players and saying, 'This is the game.' I'm disappointed that we didn't give a better showing in Wanganui, but this is the game. After the Auckland Test I'm saying to my side, 'You can beat them. Just given five days of fair weather, you're going to beat them.' John Emburey and I are picking them up all the time. In racehorse terms, we're getting them ready for the race. They've had a 'prep' and now there's a big one coming up.

We've made two changes to our team from Auckland. Caddick comes in for Mullally, maybe to bowl a stricter line, and Croft for White, to give us the balance of the five-man attack with plenty of options. Robert Croft has been terrific in the way he accepted the tactical decision not to play him in the First Test. In hindsight it might have been the wrong decision, but we were pushed that way by the Auckland preparations and the pitch. New Zealand have brought in a fast bowler, Geoff Allott, and a left-arm spinner, the 18-year-old Daniel Vettori, for Vaughan and Morrison.

In my job I'm conscious that you don't get involved with other people's sides, but I saw Vettori in England when he was with the under-19 tour last year. And when they were manoeuvring towards a Test team, with the Select team at Palmerston North, and they were trying a chap called Haslam, I thought, 'He's twice as good, is Vettori.' Obviously their selectors at last recognised the fact and pitched him in. He's got glasses, long hair, looks ungainly and reminds me so much of the young Ray East. He's got a snappy bowling action and he is to show that he does not get fazed by the occasion.

144

JA

A tiresome southerly change has brought with it a stiff, chilly wind and showers to delay the start of play on the first day until mid-afternoon. By then only thirty overs remain in the day and I am surprised when, having won the toss, Lee Germon decides to bat first. The pitch has been under a tarpaulin for twenty-four hours, and although it's cold there is enough moisture in the air to suggest that the ball might move around. Also I have witnessed several occasions in county cricket when, having sat about for much of the day, the team which eventually batted first often collapsed. It is difficult, mentally, to switch on again and inevitably you feel rather sluggish. The fielding team, on the other hand, can regroup together and the fast bowlers know that they will only have one good burst each before the close of play.

DL

Our plan has been to bat first if we win the toss and the game can start at any reasonable time. That's a consensus decision in the team. But as it goes on and the delay for the rain gets longer, it begins to look as if there might be an uncomfortable hour and a half or two hours and we're rethinking. It's a no-win situation here. We'll bowl.

When the captain goes out at last for the toss, he announces to the team, 'They've won the toss and they're batting. I would have batted as well.' I always go out to the toss these days, because the captain gets delayed by interviews, someone's got to get the news back to the dressing room quickly and it might as well be me.

This time the coin has gone up and Germon has won it and confidently said, 'We'll have a bat.' But you could see in his eyes and in the shape of his shoulders that he didn't want to win the toss. He didn't want to make that decision. So I play on that when I'm back in the dressing room. 'He's won it and he didn't want to win it. He's batting and he didn't really want to bat.'

Now New Zealand have got that uncomfortable no-win

situation for a batting side. It only needs a couple of wickets. That would be plenty and you'd be back into them the morning after with another fresh session. So we're very eager to get out there.

JA

After those thirty overs, New Zealand are all but out of the match at 56 for 6. Darren Gough has taken 3 for 12 from eight overs and Andy Caddick 3 for 19. Wickets have tumbled spectacularly, all to catches, and although the ball has done just enough off the seam to give the bowlers encouragement, New Zealand's batting is woefully undisciplined.

We also witness the beginning of Dominic Cork's sad fall from grace. From the distance of the commentary box, he appears to suggest to the umpires, after an over or two, that the bowler's run-up at his end is unfit for play. Given the fact that he has been given – wrongly in my opinion – the stiff wind behind him and has all the conditions in his favour, it is an extraordinarily eccentric performance. Atherton does exactly the right thing and takes him off. Replaced by Gough, Cork stands in the gully and watches as the Yorkshireman tears in wholeheartedly and picks up his rewards.

DL

The problem seems to be that the mechanism for the stump camera is buried behind the stumps, but to one side, right on the right-arm over-the-wicket bowler's run-up, and it's then filled in with a sandy base and there's a couple of sods of turf on top. And Dominic Cork has trouble getting his footing just at that point. So he's come off, but it means that Darren Gough comes on earlier than would have been anticipated, and he just hits his straps and looks in good rhythm and good pace.

I've felt that they're worried about Darren and they're worried about his pace. That's what's disturbing them. He's a stocky lad, with a pumping action. It's all action, but he does generate decent pace and he's getting the ball through. He bowls either a full or a short length and they've not really come to terms with him. Now he's bowling in tandem with Caddick and it's a good mix. Gough is bustle and Caddick with his height has that probing line and length. The pitch is dry, but it's been covered and there's moisture around. There's bound to be something in it.

Caddick bowls a natural 'back of a length'. He's got bounce with his height, and if he gets it in the right place people will always say that he looks a Test Match bowler. He's always there. Andrew's basically shy, but he's a grand lad.

The worry now is Dominic Cork and we recognise that it's just not coming out right for him. He's a pitch-it-up swing bowler, nip-it-away, hustle the batsman, and it's just not happening. The disappointment is obviously the team's, but it's his as well and he shows it more than most.

Caddick and Gough have shared the wickets and it's a terrific start. 56 for 6! We're absolutely in 'em. We've done that day's work. Tomorrow morning we can roll 'em over.

JA

It takes England only an hour and a half to finish off the innings, bowling New Zealand out for a paltry 124. Nathan Astle makes 36 and Dipak Patel, coming in at number 8, a more than useful 45, but Gough and Caddick, again, are on target and, backed up by some terrific close-in fielding, New Zealand are not allowed to slip out of the noose. Gough finishes with five for 40 and Caddick, in his first Test of the tour, four for 45.

The only chance New Zealand have of staying in the game is to take early wickets and, in the third over, Nick Knight cuts firmly and is caught at point off Doull for 8. But the rest of the day belongs to England. Atherton and Stewart put on 70 for the second wicket before the captain is adjudged lbw to the perservering Doull for 30, and it takes a brilliant diving left-handed low catch at first slip by Fleming to dismiss Stewart off Allott for 52. At the close, England are already 80 runs in the lead at 204 for 3. Chris Cairns, who is every bit as much an actor as Cork, has damaged a finger on his right hand. Checks confirm that it is not broken, which suggests that he should be able to bowl again later in the match. However, Cairns and three team-mates decide that an evening out is in order and, next morning, a radio phone-in programme receives a call from a taxi driver who claims to have dropped Cairns back at his hotel at 4 a.m.

The New Zealand public, not to mention the media, are outraged. The cricket team has a poor record in terms of both results and discipline. Patience is running thin. Cairns, of course, had prematurely left a recent tour of the West Indies under a cloud – a falling out with the then manager Glenn Turner was cited as a reason for that – and with New Zealand in such a desperate position in this match, plus the fact that they face a long and crucial following day in the field, many pundits decide that enough is enough.

The matter is also handled clumsily by the home authorities, who, despite repeated requests, refuse to name any of the players involved, thereby implicating everybody. They will also not reveal what action, if any, has been taken. Christopher Doig, the opera-singing chief executive, puts in a particularly pompous performance in the press box which settles nothing, so the arguments continue to rage in the media.

The one thing that a struggling team cannot afford to do is to give any impression at all that they are not properly prepared. The public have every right to be incensed, and that feeling of frustration grows all the more when Cairns does not bowl a single delivery on the third day, which he spends in the dressing-room.

DL
We gradually get wind of this story. We're getting on with the game, but you can tell that there are little meetings going on here and there with little press conferences arranged.

148

Then there are statements coming out and we've nothing to add and it's turmoil for all concerned. It comes out that they may not have been as professional as they should, and we're just getting on with the job. The funny thing is that they think they're getting some negative press. That's nothing. It's Enid Blyton stuff compared with what we get. It must be a distraction for them. It's a similar distraction to the one we had at The Oval last year, when we had a problem with Chris Lewis and we announced that he'd been left out of the one-day squad while the Test was going on. That overtakes the game. So they must be on the back foot through that.

JA

Meanwhile, Graham Thorpe takes full advantage and scores 108, his second consecutive Test century, in five and a half hours. He has been dropped in the gully on 39, but this is further evidence of the growth in confidence of a batsman who never had any problem reaching 50, but appeared to have a mental block in converting those scores into centuries. Hopefully the tide has now turned.

DL

Graham Thorpe is a lovely touch player. I'm a bit biased when they're left-handed and playing well, because I was a left-handed batsman, but I like watching him play. But sometimes I just think, 'Don't hit him there, hit him here', particularly against Vettori. But that's different styles of play. He is a busy player and he's a touch player. In Zimbabwe, with the slowness of the pitches there and the deadness of the outfields, the touch players did struggle, because they had no pace from the ball. Now here they've got pace off the ball and they come into their own.

JA

Thorpe and Nasser Hussain (64) take their overnight partnership to 107 before Hussain becomes Vettori's first Test victim, caught by Young at slip. The youngster, who reminds me of the murdered Angie Dickinson's son in the Michael Caine film *Dressed to Kill*, bowls every bit as well as I knew he would. Some people are mature enough at 18 to make the giant step up to international cricket, while others are not. Vettori appears to be about as laid back as you can be, and, when he nips out Caddick to finish with 2 for 98 from 34.3 overs, he has more than justified his controversial selection.

Thorpe and Crawley add 118 for the fifth wicket to extend England's lead to 207, Crawley making 56, patiently, in three hours. Any worries anyone might have had about England delaying their declaration are blown away as they lose their last six wickets for 52 runs to be bowled out for 383. I am sure they will be disappointed about that, but their lead is 259 and I reckon they have done themselves a favour in giving themselves plenty of time to dismiss New Zealand a second time and win the match.

DL

We don't get enough down the order, which does irritate me, but there's a little flurry right at the end between Caddick and Tuffers which adds 26 for the last wicket. Tuffers continues his rich vein of form with 6 not out and Caddick makes a useful 20.

We've got a great lead even though people might say, 'Well, why didn't you get a few more?' It's healthy and you'd reckon that there's only one winner here. Still, we've got some work to do.

JA

To give New Zealand's openers full credit, Pocock and Young survive a potentially testing 21 overs and some increasingly hysterical English appealing to finish the third day at 48 without loss.

Next day, though, one look out of my hotel room window tells me that we are in for another rain-affected day. The flags on top of the old dockside buildings are barely still attached to their poles as the furious southerly hurries in a succession of squally showers. When I arrive at the Basin Reserve, it is clear that we are in for another lengthy delay. Radio New Zealand do not have a problem at moments such as this. They throw open their phone lines for their 'Daily Keno Sports Talk: You call the shots', which, punctuated with scores of advertisements, happily passes the time as the listeners queue up to have their say. There is no shortage of material at the moment, with the 'Late Night Out Saga' still attracting plenty of space in the newspapers.

That is all well and good, but what about poor old 'Test Match Special', which is taking the commentary directly from Radio New Zealand? How on earth will Peter Baxter fill the time in a lonely little studio in London? I make one or two enquiries and establish that it is possible for the phone-in to be relayed to the UK. But what about the adverts which keep Radio New Zealand viable? Even though an advert for a particular brand of New Zealand toilet paper would not be of any interest to 'TMS' listeners, it must not be broadcast on the BBC.

Eventually, with Bryan Waddle's help, we strike a deal. No adverts will be played for forty-five minutes and the programme can be relayed to the UK. Peter Baxter appears to be somewhat relieved when I pass on the news, and we go on the air. By the time 'TMS' listeners have joined us, the phone-in is in full swing and a number of New Zealand sports fans are having their say. Waddle gives out the telephone number once or twice, and it is not long before we hear the producer saying, 'Next caller: Dennis from Southport. Where's that?' The first of our listeners has got through. Peter Baxter telephones my mobile. 'Get Waddle to give out the number again,' he urges. 'They're jamming the switchboard in Broadcasting House!' From that moment on, New Zealand callers are comfortably outnumbered by those who dial in from the UK. It is extraordinary, and reassuring to know that people at home are actually tuning in. My favourite call comes from Elizabeth, a rugby fan in Ashby de la Zouch.

'Hello, Jonathan?'

'Hello, Elizabeth. How are things in Leicestershire tonight? You're making me feel very homesick, you know!'

'We won!'

'Sorry?'

'We won!'

'Who won?'

'The Tigers. We beat Bath at the Recreation Ground this afternoon.'

'Brilliant! Now what's your point?'

'Nothing! That's all I wanted to tell you!'

'Goodnight, Elizabeth!'

Callers come through from all over the UK. The deluge is so great that the phone-in swiftly becomes titled the 'International Daily Keno phone-in' and not a single advert is played for over an hour.

Eventually, play is able to start after lunch with forty-nine overs remaining, and until the last half hour New Zealand give themselves an excellent chance of saving the match. Pocock and Young put on 89 for the first wicket, at which point Young edges Tufnell to Stewart for 64. Adam Parore, under huge pressure, and Pocock hang around for another hour and fifty minutes before Robert Croft changes the whole balance of the day.

DL

Parore is lbw to Croft's arm ball. The next man in is Stephen Fleming, who gets under pressure with an attacking field around him. There's no time left in the day and he just needs to survive. He just needs to get through to the close. But you can tell the application of the pressure. He's like a cat on hot bricks. He's moving all the time. He's moving out to square leg, then coming back in. He's not composed. And then he plays this horrendous shot, looking to hit Croft over the mid-wicket area. The batter would say he is trying to hit it straight, but he shapes over mid-wicket. It ends up as a high ball that Croft calls for himself. Caught and bowled for 0. Now, that's a big wicket – Stephen Fleming, a good player of spin – at the end of the day. But we haven't finished. There's a night-watchman in, Dipak Patel, who doesn't want to play with the bat – he kicks one away and he's lbw as well. So, from the game going nowhere, with both openers still there, in the space of a few overs we've nicked four out. It's 125 for 4; they're still 134 behind and we're in the ascendancy.

JA

In his last five overs before the end of the fourth day, Croft has taken 3 for 0 – 3 for 12 from 16 overs in the innings. Mike Atherton has suddenly discovered the benefits of crowding the bat and England are on the verge of victory. With the bad weather that has been around, there is enormous relief when the final day dawns dry and bright.

DL

Seventy-three overs have been bowled in this innings and we are due a new ball at eighty, so we're in a great position. It's dictated for us. We'll start with the spinners. They're the ones that did the damage last night. We'll get pressure on again; men round the bat. They can bowl four overs apiece and see how it goes. If it doesn't work, we can take the new ball straight away. It's perfect.

The spinners don't take a wicket. Germon, the captain, is in, with the opening batsman, Pocock. Gough comes on and bowls Germon off an inside edge and so we're off again. They're 161 for 5. They've had a nightwatchman in, which has pushed the batters further down the order, so we've still work to do, with Nathan Astle and Chris Cairns to come in.

But Goughie is striking now. He's taken one wicket. He's got a new ball. He's steaming in, in true Fred Trueman tradi-tion. Pocock plays a loose shot and gets a nick and Nick Knight looks as if he's taking the catch in slow motion above his head. But it's an absolutely stunning catch. It's one of eleven he takes in the five Tests on this tour. It gives the bowlers so much confidence to look at that slip cordon:

Thorpe, Knight, Hussain, Atherton. That's as good as any. They don't miss any.

Now Gough's got rid of the opener. Astle can hold us up – we've not really come to terms with how to get him out because he plays that many shots. He's miss one, hit one, miss one, miss one, hit one, but this time we've got him in against the new ball. He falls to a wonderful catch from a top wicket-keeper. Stewart's committed himself and taken the responsibility, diving in front of slip, and just caught it in the webbing of the glove. Gough's gone bang, bang, bang – and they're reeling now. I can see in the eyes in their dressing room, they're down and out. We're thinking: well, there's no Danny Morrison here this time.

Darren Gough gets Doull caught again by Knight at second slip and Andy Caddick gets the last two, and we've steam-rollered them in little more than a session. We've won by an innings and 68 runs. It's a great win.

JA

Looking at the players, as they celebrate wildly on their dressing room balcony by spraying champagne Formula One-style, it is as if they have won the Ashes rather than beating this poor New Zealand outfit. But it is relief they are experiencing, more than anything else. Finally, after the disappointments which have dogged the tour up to now, they are winners; and they are clearly going to enjoy every moment.

We are busy too. My hotel telephone rings all evening with requests for appearances on innumerable radio stations back home. It is a pleasure to do them all. Too often during my time in this job I have been the harbinger of bad news, both on and off the field. This is only the fifth England victory I have witnessed overseas since my first tour in 1990, and I really believe that we, the press, get almost as much of a thrill out of it as the players themselves.

DL

Darren Gough, 9 for 92 in the match, was on fire on the field and he is on fire in the dressing room. All you can hear there is, 'Nine for me, just the nine, nine for me.' He's not won the Man of the Match award, though. I probably would have given it to him, but it's gone to Thorpey, who did play a super innings.

The music's on. We're all hugging each other. It's a Test Match win after a lot of frustration and a lot of hard work. John Crawley knocks the music off. So it's dead quiet. 'What's happened?'

He says, 'You've got to close your coffin lids', referring to the big cases we carry the cricket kit in. 'Everybody close their coffin lids.'

There are cries of 'What's he on about?'

He says, 'Well, when you win big matches there's always somebody spraying champagne about and it gets all over your clothes and they're wet and they smell. Now, we know a lot about that at Lancashire. It's a regular occurrence at Old Trafford. A lot of you won't know anything about it.' They drown him for that, of course, but it is a great line.

There are lots and lots of songs and when Lord MacLaurin comes in he gets 'We've all been to Tesco's, We've all been to Tesco's, La la la la … La la la …' So we're in good spirits and we continue with it back at the hotel. We have a team meeting impromptu, up in the manager's room, with everybody gathered there and having some terrific fun. And all those supporters of ours have now got a spring in their step. It's us that matters; we're the team, but there's relief from those spectators. Suddenly they're not looking at us as if we've got two heads. 'Well done, great performance.'

'Thanks ever so much. I hope you've enjoyed it.' Because that's what they're here to do, to enjoy the cricket.

There is, of course, a feeling of relief. We're on tour, we're away from home, we know that we're going in the right direction and it has just needed a win. Now there is the relief of having played well and, despite the amount of time that's been taken out of the game, we've given a terrific performance from start to finish, with our bowlers on top and our batsmen turning the screw and getting a good total on the board and then going to work and bowling out the opposition again. I've identified this need for a cutting edge to bowl sides out twice. Sometimes it will take us longer than teams like Pakistan, because we don't have Wasim Akram and Waqar Younis, or Australia, because we don't have Shane Warne. Nevertheless, we are bowling teams out at Test Match level, which is good.

After we've won, I've stayed away from the press conference. Now they'll want to talk to the players who won the game. I've taken the flak when we haven't been doing so well. That's just the way it is. I suppose it goes with the territory. That's out of my control, I just get on with my job.

16

CHRISTCHURCH: CAPTAIN'S MATCH

DAVID LLOYD

We arrive in the lovely city of Christchurch, and Ian Botham has organised fishing. We're going up into the hills. We've got two cars organised and we're going game-fishing – salmon, sea trout, the lot. It's absolutely pouring down. It never looks like stopping. We go up to a sheep farm and we're splendidly entertained by the farmer and his family. It's a gorgeous place, with a lake outside his front door.

We've got a few novice fishermen with us, who are anxious to get going. Beefy and I don't bother. We'll sit here with a glass of wine and a cup of tea and maybe another glass of wine. We move on further up into the hills, where there's a lodge. It's really remote and there's a river and a stream. Our novices are off fishing again and it's still lagging down and they've hardly any waterproofs or any of the right gear. Beefy says to me, 'We're not going, are we?'

'No, we'll stay here.'

'That's good,' he says. 'I've just brought these bottles of wine. We'll get the logs on this fire going. Get that settee round here in front of the fire.' So we get the fire blazing, with the settee in front of it and he and I set about demolishing the bottles of wine, while the rain lashes down on the mad fishermen outside.

When we leave, we're slumped in the back of the car and we're due to stop off at a place where somebody has said, 'Just drop the lads in. It'll be very informal, but we'll have a drink and a bit of a barbecue.' We turn up at this place and find a car park for a hundred. The Lord Mayor's there and we're in shorts and no shoes. 'Sorry, we can't stay. We're improperly dressed. It wasn't quite what we were expecting. I hope you won't mind if we carry on back.' So that's what we have to do.

After a long sleep, I realise I've been well and truly Bothamed. You do hear stories about that happening to people who find that they've lost half a day of their lives. But now we're ready for some hard preparation for the Third Test here in Christchurch.

JONATHAN AGNEW

Christchurch is one of the most beautiful and peaceful cities on the cricket circuit. It is probably more English than anywhere in England itself, and the avenues of weeping willow trees dripping their long branches into the meandering River Avon are stunning. You can hire a punt along the Avon, which is a thoroughly relaxing experience; the only drawback being that you have to beat off at least 200 Japanese tourists first!

What a pity, then, that Lancaster Park is so featureless. Like most of the cricket grounds in New Zealand, it is primarily a rugby stadium with ugly terracing all round one side. At least, now, there is the splendid Hadlee stand, which is a tribute to the entire family, not just Sir Richard, and which is positioned just to the right of the media area. And, of course, there are the new floodlights.

And new is the word. Imagine building a floodlight tower with a Meccano set and you would not be far wrong. The most intriguing thing of all is that the lights are hung on a horizontal rather than vertical platform, which is the more common practice. It will be fascinating to see how effective they are during the one-day international which follows this Test Match.

Following their very good win in Wellington, everyone will be hoping – and wanting – England to come out and do the same thing here. That they are the better team is not in doubt, but England are striving for greater consistency in Test cricket, and this seems like a very good place to start. New Zealand, on the other hand, have all sorts of problems. Their major sponsor, a brewery, has been making threatening noises following the late-night-out episode, and the Bank of New Zealand, which sponsors the Test series, is also chuntering. Worse still, Lee Germon, the captain, is ruled out with a groin strain, so Stephen Fleming becomes New Zealand's youngest-ever Test captain. With his team one down and just this one match left to play, he faces something of a challenge.

DL

New Zealand now look a better-balanced side. Parore, who might have lost his place in the side, stays to keep wicket, but they have brought two new faces in for Germon and Dipak Patel. Matt Horne is in for his first Test. He's a nice lad. We've played against him in a couple of games and he's an attacking batsman; a confident lad. And Heath Davis – known as 'Starkers' or 'Ravers', who took six wickets against us at Wanganui, is in the side. He's eccentric, to say the least, but we're really warming to him. He's a top lad, a really grand lad. They've talked him up a lot. 'He's a really fast bowler.' Well, he's not fast. He's pacey, but he's not going to frighten anybody. But he gets it straight now, which he didn't do when he was in England on their last tour there.

Even when we're playing Test Matches, I can feel a respect from both sides. It's hammer and tongs stuff, as it should be, but there's a respect for each other. They're easy in each other's company, by and large. They've got some terrific lads all through the side.

The pitch is green. There's that suggestion of a lack of preparation and a bit of moisture. If there's going to be anything in it, it'll be in it now. You get all this from the groundsman again. They're dead honest here. We feel if we can nip three out on the first morning, we can work away from there and it'll be a better batting pitch as the match goes on. And so, when we win the toss, we put them in. We're never afraid to say, 'Well, you can have a bat. We'll bowl you out.'

As it is, they're only two wickets down by lunch, four down at tea and 229 for 5 at the end of the first day. We have had a catch dropped towards the end of the day, which would have made it six down, which is what it really should be after putting them in. Again it's Croft who's applied pressure in taking three wickets – 3 for 49 from 24 overs. Cork and Gough have the other two. Matt Horne has got a cracked wrist, though he has carried on to get 42 in his first Test innings, and the new captain, Fleming, has been stumped off Croft in the last hour and that's always a big wicket. So 229 for 5 is not the end of the world. We're in control with the score, but we probably needed another wicket to say, 'Well, that's a damn good day. We can bowl 'em out for 280.'

JA

Although it is fifty-five minutes before they make a breakthrough, the second morning belongs to England. Parore is beautifully taken low at slip, once again by Hussain, for 59, and he is followed by one of the most remarkable run-outs I am ever likely to see. Cairns plays a no-ball from Cork into the on side and calls a disbelieving Doull for a run. There, lurking at widish mid-on, is none other than Phil Tufnell, who comes darting in and not only manages to pick up the ball cleanly but, with an action not dissimilar to Clive Lloyd in his heyday, plucks out the middle stump with a direct throw. A replay is called for (Tufnell tells me later that he felt rather embarrassed at this juncture because he did not know what to do with himself while England were all waiting for the third umpire to make up his mind) and, finally, Doull is ruled to be out. In the commentary box, we are unanimous: the champagne moment is immediately awarded to Tufnell which, before lunch on the second day, is the earliest the award has ever been handed out.

DL

It's been my aim to encourage all of our lads to be aggressive in the field. Now, we're aggressive behind the stumps, because of the catching. We can get more aggressive in the outfield by shying at the stumps. Throw the stumps down; make the non-striker get back; prevent the leisurely stroll. So we do a little bit of shying at the stumps. Sometimes it's not absolutely necessary, but on this occasion Tufnell has pounced on the ball, picked up one-handed and thrown the stumps down to run out Doull, who's a fast runner. That, to me, is very special. Tuffers is quietly satisfied and the lads all respond to him. He's the centre of attention. He's been terrific all tour. He's complemented Croft. They've bowled well in tandem. He's done everything that's been required of him in fitness and I think he finds that not the easiest thing to do. He's been an excellent tourist and not a problem to anybody.

JA

England's morning is completed by the dismissal of Cairns, caught behind off Caddick, for a determined 57, and at lunch New Zealand are 314 for 8. Daniel Vettori once again shows his maturity – and very good reason for moving a place or two up the order – by scoring 25 as he and the unlikely Heath Davis add 27 for the ninth wicket. But when Hussain takes his third catch off Croft to dismiss Davis for 8 – and give Croft his best Test figures of 5 for 95 from 39.1 overs – New Zealand are all out for 346.

DL

Robert Croft continues to get rave reports. It's the way that he bowls, the line that he bowls and the spin that he imparts. And he finds the pace. I think that it's been good for him that he's got Tufnell with him as a pair. He is a thinker about the game, the life and soul of the dressing room, but a strong competitor, and he talks all the time with John Emburey – nothing more than just chatting it through. 'It's coming out well. Your pace was right, perhaps it could have been a bit quicker.' That's been a big plus for us on this tour, having two coaches.

Off-spinners have been becoming a little unfashionable in Test cricket, but there's evidence now that they are coming back, with Muralitharan and Saqlain. What irks me ever so slightly is that they're talked of as 'the best'. They've got to be something, if they're better than Croft. He's as good as any of them, if not better. Now I'm a big believer in shouting about our top players from the rooftops. He's very similar to a latter-day Fred Titmus and, more recently, Tim May. He's strong in temperament and he gets better and better. The rave reports he gets are pleasing for us, because we've selected him and he's shown he can do it.

JA

The pitch is still very easy-paced and full of runs, so England's reply is most disappointing. Knight edges Allott to Fleming at slip for 14. Stewart, after a cavalier start, is caught in the gully – again off the left-armer – for 15. And when Hussain, on 12, nicks Cairns through to Parore, England are 70 for 3.

Atherton drops anchor at the other end to play another of those backs-to-the-wall innings he thrives upon. But when he loses Thorpe, bowled by Astle for 18, and Crawley, caught behind for 1, in consecutive overs with England still 266 runs behind, the captain is quickly running out of partners. England's batsmen seem to play with the attitude of 'Oh well, if I don't get any, someone else will'. With the result that at the end of the second day they are 145 for 5 and the series hangs in the balance.

DL

Nobody's really got going, except Atherton, who's still there on 66. That, at least, is a big bonus for us. New Zealand have got rid of all but one of our specialist batsmen and we've not got 150. I'm disappointed with the way we've played, but we've got to play round the captain now.

JA

A cheery soul picks me up in a taxi outside my hotel this morning and quickly gets on to the subject of cricket. He turns out to be Dick Motz, the former New Zealand seam bowler who toured England twice and who was the first Kiwi to take a hundred Test wickets. We agree that it is vital from England's perspective that Cork, who has 16, gets his head down and supports Atherton. Otherwise New Zealand will be firmly in control.

To the fifth ball of the morning Cork plays a wild pull shot at Davis and is caught by Parore. It is the worst possible start for England, and it's difficult to work out what on earth Cork was thinking of. However, Croft digs in to play another of his gutsy innings, which takes England past the follow-on and Atherton to within sight of another century. The pair have put on 53 for the seventh wicket when Croft, 31, receives a slow full-toss from Astle. Apparently caught in that old predicament of not knowing whether to hit it for 4 or 6, Croft instead spoons a catch to mid-on and walks off shaking his head in bewilderment.

Now Atherton's century is seriously threatened.

Gough misses a delivery from Vettori, which is as straight as a gun barrel, and is bowled for 0, and Caddick falls to Allott, now armed with the second new ball. England are 210 for 9, and Atherton is 92 not out as Tufnell strides purposefully to the crease. As is always the case at moments such as this, there is a flurry of activity from the scorers in the commentary boxes. 'How many Englishmen have carried their bats through completed innings in Test cricket?' we ask. The answer is that 33 batsmen have achieved that feat in Test history, six of them being Englishmen, with Len Hutton managing it twice.

Two glorious cover drives from Tufnell add to the excitement but, on 13, he edges Doull to Young at second slip and Atherton, having defended stoutly for five hours and 48 minutes, is left stranded on 94. He has the consolation of joining Hutton and co. in *Wisden*, but England's batting performance has been curiously flimsy and New Zealand have a lead of 118.

DL

We're not in an ideal situation, to say the least, but they've got to put that behind them and go and bowl them out again. There's still bags of time left in the game, midway through the third day, and now the captain comes into his own. He rallies the troops. 'We're not saving this game. We're going to win it. We're going to bowl them out. We've done it before and we're going to do it again.' He's got everybody fired up and we coaches can sit back. All the positive things are coming out. 'We're better than they are. We're going to win the game.'

JA

Fifty-three overs remain to be bowled in the day and, as he has in the first innings, Cork strikes immediately, bowling Pocock with only his fourth delivery. A rare lapse by Knight at slip in Caddick's opening over allows Young a let-off but, with the last ball before tea, Gough finds the edge of Parore's bat to give Stewart his fourteenth dismissal of the series: a record for an English wicket-keeper against New Zealand. It is now 42 for 2, New Zealand lead by 160, but after the interval, during a tense and often ill-tempered final session, we witness a startling collapse which completely turns the game on its head and throws the Radio New Zealand commentary box into silence.

Young and Fleming take the score on to 61 and the lead to 179 when Fleming is caught at silly-point by Knight off

Tufnell for 11. Astle follows, 15 runs later, to the familiar Hussain/Croft combination, but it is when the score is 80 for 4 that we witness an extraordinary incident.

Tufnell bowls to Young, who, having batted for nearly three hours, plays forward. The ball definitely flicks the edge of the bat and loops off the front pad towards Knight, who is standing very close in on the off side. Knight dives forwards with a scooping motion, and claims that he takes a catch with the ball only millimetres off the ground. The other fielders in the vicinity join in with the appeal.

Umpire Darryl Hair, no stranger to controversy, waits for a moment before raising his finger. Young is out. The batsman has other ideas, however. Slow-motion replays show him saying to Knight: 'No way! You didn't catch that.' He does not move from the crease. Now Hair is pressured into making a mistake. He strolls over to his colleague at square leg, Stephen Dunne, the New Zealander, who ironically had been the umpire who appeared not to support Hair when he no-balled the Sri Lankan off-spinner, Muralitharan, in Australia the winter before. A brief discussion takes place before Hair, once again, raises his finger. Mortified, Young troops off as England celebrate.

From the sidelines, it has looked dreadful. However, Young later escapes punishment from the referee, Peter Burge, because he claims that he did not see Hair give him out. Meanwhile replays confirm that Young, who had scored 49, might have been unlucky. It was a dreadfully difficult decision for Hair to have made; a few years ago one of the close fielders might have pointed to the ground and helped the umpire but, sadly, that level of sportsmanship has long gone. Nevertheless, Hair should not have involved the square-leg umpire because he had already made up his mind. It would have set a very dangerous precedent if he had altered his decision, because the batsman had appeared to refuse to go. England are delighted. New Zealand are 80 for 5 and they lose another wicket, Simon Doull, before the close to finish the day on 95 for 6. They have done their best to throw the Test Match away.

DL

We've just gone through them. That first wicket for Dominic Cork, bowling Pocock, has given everybody a lift at the start of the innings. Now 95 for 6 means that we're achieving exactly what we set out to do. Now we've got to get them out as quickly as possible. New Zealand's lead is already 213 and I'm asked in a close-of-play interview what sort of target we would not want to have to chase. My reply is, '330 would be a big ask. 280 would be terrific and 300 won't be the end of the world.'

JA

This Test match is building up to a thrilling finish. The fourth morning is crucial as New Zealand, led by Cairns and Horne, bravely batting with his broken hand, try to score another 100 runs or so. England need to wrap up the innings as quickly as possible. Horne survives four overs before edging Caddick to Stewart, but Vettori plays extremely well and England are not helped when Stewart fumbles a stumping chance, offered by Cairns, when he has 31.

The lead grows. Cairns is missed again when he has 51; dropped by Cork at mid-off when the lead is 291, but, five runs later, Cairns throws away all his hard work by smashing Tufnell out to deep extra-cover where Knight takes a catch only yards inside the boundary. Although he has played a terrific innings of 52, it seems such a waste because the job has not been completed. He and Vettori have added 71 crucial runs and when Gough mops up Davis and Allott on the stroke of lunch, New Zealand are 186 all out. England need 305 to win the match. Only once have they ever managed to score more than 300 to win a Test – and that was seven years ago.

166

DL

I said yesterday that 330 would be a big ask. It's 305. All we need is sixty a session. There's no need to do anything untoward. We get a start. When you're 60 for no wicket, you can say, 'Right, we only need 240. Bags of time. Keep going. Keep your nerve.' Shot selection comes into it. There'll be a lot happening out there. They've got to block it all out and keep their nerve.

There's so much rough outside the right-hander's leg stump that the left-arm spin bowler can't miss it.

JA

Vettori holds the key to the outcome of the series. It might seem terribly unfair to burden such a young man with that level of responsibility, but there is a great deal of rough outside the leg stump, Vettori is the only spinner in the New Zealand team, so that is the situation in which he finds himself. How will he cope with the pressure?

In fact, he takes the first wicket when Knight lofts a catch to Davis at mid-on. Knight has made 29 and the total is 64. There is still a long way to go. New Zealand decide, quite rightly, that Vettori is going to bowl into the rough in an attempt to reduce England's chances of scoring. This is best illustrated by Stewart's innings. Normally such a free-scoring batsman, he makes only 17 in 108 minutes before Vettori cunningly changes the angle and switches to round the wicket. Stewart pops up a catch to Pocock at short leg. 116 for 2.

Atherton, who on 55 must have been perilously close to being lbw to Astle, is still there at the close with 65. Caddick, the nightwatchman, has joined him and England need a further 187 with eight wickets in hand to win the match on what promises to be a nerve-jangling final day.

DL

We have had a number of nightwatchmen ready in the dressing room. We would have sent in one after another if another wicket had gone down at the end. Tufnell was the next one padded up.

We still need sixty a session. We're on course. But some of the pundits are saying, 'It's been turgid, the way England have approached this. They've got to be more positive.' You couldn't miss that patch of rough and Vettori's bowled over the wicket almost exclusively. He's just dropped the ball into it, and with a leg-side field you've either got to kick it or wait for him to miss it, cut it or, if he bowls a full toss, knock that away. There are no other scoring options. It's just too unpredictable in that area. It's just rutted footmarks.

Now some people are telling us, after that fourth day, 'What they've got to do is get down the pitch, get leg-side of the ball and hit it over extra cover. Now that's the way to play on this pitch.' So next morning, early, I get them in the nets. I get two of the bowlers with big boots and ask them to rip up this area just outside that leg stump, just like the patch out in the middle.

We've got two slow left-arm bowlers. Tuffers is a Test Match bowler, and the other one is me. I say to them, 'Right, I want you to hit these over extra cover.' They look at me strangely. I say, 'Well, this is how one or two Test players of yesteryear would have played on this, although nobody bowled left-arm over-the-wicket, as far as I'm aware. But come on, let's see who can do it. I'm fifty. I haven't bowled since 1980 and I weren't very good when I did that.' And not one of them – top batters – get it there. We have a bit of fun. That's all we're doing. It takes the heat out of it.

'That's what you're going to get all day. You've got to have a game plan and I hope that's not in your game plan. We carry on. We need sixty a session. There's runs to be had at the other end. Keep this guy out – that's the danger. You'll be kicking it for ever. It looks ugly, but there's a game on. There's a game to win, not to draw.' After all, they can't afford to be too defensive, and the other thing is, how long can this lad Vettori carry on? He's never been in the realms of forty and fifty overs before.

JA

My day starts early with a trip to the domestic terminal at Christchurch airport to meet my wife, Emma. Despite having flown all the way from England – twenty-nine hours in total – she is in surprisingly good form and agrees that she should come directly to Lancaster Park where a great day is in prospect.

New Zealand urgently need a couple of early wickets, particularly Atherton's, if they are to cause a panic. However, Caddick survives for fifty minutes, scoring 15, and his is the only wicket England lose before lunch. It has been a vital session.

DL

Caddick may only have scored 15, but he has hit a square-leg six, which has given us all a lift. He's hung about, too, and while he's been there Atherton's moved on to 75. Twenty-five minutes before lunch, they've taken the new ball and that helps us. Captain and vice-captain are in now. They've got us to lunch at 203 for 3 and now we only need 102 more with seven wickets left. We're in a good position, but fully aware that one wicket often brings two, brings three. You've got to see it through yourself. The responsibility is yours.

Atherton has reached his hundred before lunch, and forty minutes afterwards he and Hussain have put on 80 when he plays a loose shot to Nathan Astle; a little angled bat and a nick to the keeper. Now there might be a bit of an alarm. They've got what they wanted; they've broken the partnership.

JA

Atherton's eleventh Test century has been so richly deserved after his efforts in the first innings. Now he leaves the field for the first time in the match, nearly half-way through the last day.

Even by Atherton's standards, it has been a phenomenal

169

effort. Astle claims his wicket for 118, caught behind off an innocuous delivery, and England need only 79 more runs to win. But there is a hiccup. Four balls later, Hussain is caught by Fleming off Vettori for 33, and after five more runs have been added Thorpe gives Vettori the charge and is caught and bowled for 2. For such an accomplished player of pace bowling, his technique and his confidence against the spinners is still, surprisingly, some way behind.

DL

Hussain has got an unplayable ball from Vettori into the rough. He has tried to defend it, kick it and it has popped up and hit his glove and bounced to Fleming on the off side. Graham Thorpe has opted to come down the pitch to Vettori – nothing wrong with that – but he's stubbed his bat in the ground and lollipopped the ball back to the bowler. 226 for 3 has become 231 for 6 all of a sudden.

JA

Suddenly, New Zealand sense that they are back in the match. England need 74 to win with four wickets left. Crawley is the last of the recognised batsmen. He is joined by Cork and only Croft, Gough and Tufnell remain. The tension is excruciating.

DL

There are no cool heads in the dressing room now. Everybody's on edge. Some are in the back room, watching the TV, others are on the edges of their seats in the viewing area.

We've got Crawley and Cork in on nought and this target of 305 seems a long way away from 231 and from being absolutely flat New Zealand are buzzing. This is the position they wanted to be in. They reckon they had 300 runs to play with. England have six down and still need 76. Just four wickets to get. They just need to close in.

But our two are rock-solid. They talk it through together.

It's something we do talk about, that we play in partnerships, so when you're batting you play as a pair. That's the only team you've got out there.

JA

Twenty-six painstaking runs are added before tea, so 48 are required after the break; not enough to make time a factor, but if Vettori continues to make scoring a difficulty, then overs could start to come into the equation.

Crawley, on 20, offers a sharp chance to Pocock at short leg. Down it goes and with it goes New Zealand's last opportunity. Crawley and Cork embrace and snatch stumps when, finally, the winning runs are scored. They have put on 76 in two hours to achieve England's first consecutive victories in Test cricket since they were last in New Zealand five years ago.

DL

Crawley and Cork have inched their way home. They've played what I call real clever cricket. They haven't allowed themselves to be fazed by the situation, by the total, by the opposition or by the pitch. It's the first time England have scored as many in the fourth innings to win a Test Match since 1928–29 in Melbourne, and that was with the likes of Jack Hobbs playing. It's a terrific feeling of achievement on that pitch, and from the position we were in with the deficit on first innings, to have fought back, knocked 'em over, and then that final backs-to-the-wall inching to victory – to have won the game, not just saved it.

Athers is man of the match, of course. I can remember saying, 'He's a class act. He'll come good and when he does, someone will be on the receiving end.' In figures, he's had a terrific tour. Afterwards Steve Rixon, the New Zealand coach, admits that Athers is the one that he was worried about. He knew that he would be the one they would have to remove because his graph was in the ascendancy.

It's just one of those things that it's fashionable to knock

171

Michael Atherton. He's a friend and a colleague and he's the captain of England. I'm just mystified, because he's terrific with the team; his character is so strong; he's very much for the cause. He's got the three lions on his chest and that's everything he wants; it gives him a tremendous lift. He's just the bloke for the job, but it seems to be fashionable to give him a tremendous amount of stick and I just don't know why. He doesn't carry himself well because of his injury and the steel plate that's in his back. And that hurts and he's on medication. He can be very cutting, but he's captain and the leader and he's got a very sharp mind. And I'm on the receiving end sometimes. But we're a partnership and he knows what I'm like and that I can be a little fiery sometimes, so he calms me down on a number of occasions. People just don't know him, but this match has been his answer.

17

POP AND PYJAMAS

DAVID LLOYD

Now we're into five one-day internationals and I'm very conscious of what happened with the three one-dayers at the end of the tour of Zimbabwe. We've done so much good work in the Test Matches, now we've got to perform in these. We put a fair amount of work in and a lot of chat. Chat means nothing. They've still got to perform.

We've had a bit of an off-the-field distraction involving Philip Tufnell. He is alleged to have got up to some sort of nefarious activity in a Christchurch restaurant, but I don't give it any credence at all and it's very suspicious that there are posters up about it at the ground before nine o'clock the next morning. That seems a little orchestrated to me.

JONATHAN AGNEW

It is going to be very difficult to take the one-day series seriously. For a start, it is tacked on to the end of the tour after the Tests have finished, and while this is infinitely better than playing limited-overs cricket between Tests, I really believe that they should come first; as a warm-up for the players and spectators in the way that we have the Texaco Trophy in England. At the end of a long tour, and after back-to-back Tests, it is inevitable that everyone, and not just the players, has had enough. There have been two free days between the final Test and the first one-day match and

Emma and I have taken the opportunity to see a bit of the area. On the first day we drive north, to Kaikoura, where if you are lucky with the weather you can take a little dinghy and go whale-watching. The giant sperm-whales, which feed in the area, are often to be seen diving just a few miles off the rugged coast and we were incredibly lucky. Our guide reckons that 'something is going on "down there", a killer whale, or something', because no fewer than seventeen enormous sperm whales float all around us, rather like semi-submerged submarines. It is a glorious sight and, without doubt, the most memorable day of the tour.

The day before the match we drive in the other direction, in the company of Robin Marlar and his wife Jill, to Akaroa, which was discovered by French settlers in 1838. A French tricolour still flies proudly over the tiny harbour, set amongst the most breathtaking scenery, which we were able to enjoy despite the speed at which Robin drives!

This end-of-term feeling is even stronger on this tour because of the manner in which the five one-day matches will be played. Raucous, blaring pop music of the players' choice will be played as each batsman makes his way out to the middle and between overs. It seems that Jack Russell is the only one really to enter into the spirit of it all by choosing 'How Much is That Doggy in the Window'! I wonder if it will ever be played? I hope so. A snatch of 'Hit the Road, Jack' will, unamusingly, be used to escort a dismissed batsman back to the pavilion, and as well as the Barmy Army, who are loyally if noisily following England everywhere, we now have the Jarmy Army, a New Zealand equivalent, who are here, at Lancaster Park, wearing their pyjamas.

The fact is that this first match needs absolutely no hype at all. It is the first match to be played under floodlights in Christchurch and the 25,000 tickets were snapped up within a few days of going on sale. It seems a great shame, not to mention an extraordinary oversight, that another domestic one-day match has been played directly after the Test and so

174

the groundsman has not been able to prepare a fresh pitch. He has done his best with the rough but, even so, it is clear that the spinners will be extremely difficult to score off. New Zealand have sent Vettori home.

DL

We're playing on the same pitch. Tuffers wasn't going to play, but seeing that, he is. 'Hit that rough, Phil.'

'Thanks a lot.'

As for the razzamatazz, I think it's fine. The only change I'd make is that I wouldn't have any of the music between overs. Later I think it gets a bit nasty when England batsmen are out, with 'Return to Sender', which they don't do when the New Zealanders are out.

JA

New Zealand choose to bat first and it is a battle. Mullally, recalled to play his first match for three weeks, nips out Young for 14, but it is Tufnell who causes the most problems. He gets rid of Astle, caught by Thorpe for 50, in his first over and then chips his way through the middle order. Parore is caught and bowled for 26, Cairns caught in the deep for 15 and Fleming stumped by Stewart for 34. New Zealand slip to 148 for 5 with Tufnell finishing with his best one-day figures of 4 for 22. Harris plays some good strokes in his 48 as the return of the quicker bowlers makes scoring a bit easier, and 19 runs come from the last two overs. But even so, 222 for 6 does not seem to be enough.

New Zealand open the bowling with off-spinner Dipak Patel, the ploy which was so successful in the 1991 World Cup. He is more expensive this evening, but bowls Atherton (thankfully restored to opening the batting in the one-day stuff) for 19. Three balls later Knight edges Doull to Germon for 8 and England have slipped to 28 for 2 in the seventh over.

The next wicket does not fall until the forty-first over, and meanwhile Stewart and Thorpe produce a thrilling partnership of 170 and the game is effectively over. I feel rather sorry for the crowd, who sit very quietly as the match slips away. It is their big night and the game has not lived up to their expectations. It even drizzles. Stewart makes 81, Thorpe 82, and although Crawley and Cork fall with only half a dozen more runs to win, Croft seals the victory with two spanking boundaries.

DL

The great thing is that their batsmen have got starts, but no one's gone on further than Astle's 50, while we've had two – Stewart and Thorpe – past 80. Their stand – and it's the importance of these partnerships again – has just about got us there. When they've got out we've been slightly exposed, but nevertheless we got there, with an over to spare. A regulation one-day chase.

JA

I feel that the players' frustrations are heightened by the fact that these matches are so spread out. Next stop is Auckland, on the North Island, and the promise of a huge crowd at Eden Park.

There has been the threat of rain throughout the day. New Zealand choose to bat first, although goodness knows what prompted them to reach that decision with the rain rule being so obviously loaded in favour of the team batting second. 253 for 8 from fifty overs is a pretty good score, but New Zealand would have topped 300 if their batsmen had not continued their practice of throwing their wickets away. Young makes 46, Fleming 42, and Cairns' 79 includes three sixes which are wonderfully signalled with a final wiggle of the right ankle by the eccentric Umpire Bowden. England's bowlers are woefully off-target, delivering no fewer than twenty extra deliveries: 16 wides and 4 no-balls leaving Nasser Hussain, leading England for the first time in the place of the injured Atherton, looking completely exasperated.

DL

We always get the talk of 'What's a good score?' The answer here is '270'.

Well, 253 is quite a good score. Five an over is always quite an ask.

JA

England get away to a flier. Stewart and Knight thrash 47 off the first six overs before the long-awaited rain finally arrives and the players are forced to leave the field. They only just manage to get back on again, and how New Zealand must wish they had not. England's target is amended to 132 from 26 overs; this being a straight calculation of New Zealand's run rate. But, crazily and crucially, the fielding restrictions still have to apply for the full fifteen overs. This gives the fielding team absolutely no chance of defending their total because they are only allowed two men outside the circle, and the match is played out in gloomy silence.

DL

With that reduced target, New Zealand don't want to play. You can understand that. But the ICC match referee gets us out there. The advantage is with us with the target worked out just on scoring rate. The New Zealanders had the chance to use the system that we had in Zimbabwe, the Duckworth/Lewis tables, but they turned it down. I think that is a fairer system to both sides. The ruling on the fielding restrictions is particularly hard on New Zealand. Their other problem is that Nick Knight plays like Nick Knight.

JA

Knight finishes with 84 not out – he really does play extremely well – but the match has been reduced to such a one-sided contest that England romp home with 39 deliveries – more than six overs – to spare. As a spectacle the game is a complete farce and not what one-day cricket was

177

designed for, either from a player's point of view or from a spectator's. New Zealand should have batted second to improve their chances of winning a rain-affected match but, whatever the circumstances, the rule would still have wrecked the game.

One-day cricket has its place, and I am certainly not one of those people who blames it for England's demise in recent years. However, despite the extraordinary number of one-day matches played throughout the world in a typical year, we are still searching for a satisfactory solution for when rain interrupts a game. Here, frankly, I have found commentating on England's innings thoroughly depressing.

DL

It's been a terrific spectacle because of Nick Knight. They couldn't bowl at him and the game's over in twenty overs. We haven't needed 26. We've got lucky with the weather, but I think we'd have won it anyway because of the start we got.

JA

Checking out of my hotel the following morning, I bump into one of the England team. He had better remain nameless. 'Morning,' I say. 'Driving to Napier?'

'No, worse luck', comes the reply. 'We've got to fly.'

'You're joking! The match is not for another two days. Why don't you drive there? It only takes four hours and you can stop off on the way and see all the geysers and mud pools at Rotorua. Then you can spend the night on the shores of Lake Taupo. It's magnificent.'

'Tell me about it!' the player moans. 'I'd love to.'

'Well, come with us,' I offer. 'There's plenty of room in the back.'

'I don't think that would go down very well with the rest of the team. But thanks for the offer, Aggers.'

How sad. Why is it that England cricketers are not allowed to be individuals any more? And what chance do they have of seeing and enjoying the countries they are visiting? It was not even that they were going to have any nets in Napier. At least Emma and I are able to enjoy the drive. Rotorua is spectacular, though rather smelly, and Lake Taupo, right in the middle of the North Island, is very tranquil. This is tainted somewhat by the discovery that most of the press have not only chosen to stay in Taupo but have also selected the same hotel. Our quiet, romantic *à deux* has been put on hold.

Napier is situated in Hawkes Bay, one of New Zealand's flourishing wine-growing regions, and is a pretty little seaside town. In fact, it is completely packed out because of the match, which is to be played under floodlights at McLean Park. I have been here once before, on our previous tour in 1992, and it is the venue of one of the most unfortunate dismissals I have ever seen. It was only the second delivery of the match between England and an 'Emerging Players XI' and David Lawrence dug one in short to the New Zealand opener, Trevor Franklyn. A tall man, Franklyn was currently out of favour with the national selectors and knew that a big score against the tourists would probably get him back in the Test team.

Franklyn aimed to fend the ball away on the leg side, but it popped up in the air and gave what appeared to be a simple catch to Alec Stewart at short leg. Franklyn was distinctly unhappy when the umpire raised his finger in response to a confident appeal, and rubbed his arm pointedly as he set off towards the pavilion. This is nothing new, of course. Many a disgruntled batsman has felt inclined to inform everyone on the ground that he has received a rough decision, and we all believed this to be just another example of that distasteful practice.

However, our sympathy for Franklyn grew somewhat when the news was leaked from the home dressing room that he had been whisked away to hospital for a precautionary X-ray. One can therefore only hazard a guess at what went through the umpire's mind when the unfortunate

179

Franklyn returned shortly before lunch, his whole arm encased in plaster, brandishing an X-ray plate which revealed a break well above the left wrist. Poor Franklyn never did make it back into the New Zealand team.

I do not remember there being any lights on the ground then, but have noted throughout this trip that several day/night games are played here under what appear to be substandard floodlights. Not just that; this is the first time I have ever had to commentate from square leg. It is, literally, a brand-new ball game.

DL

It's the best pitch we've seen on the tour. Great carry and good pace. The lights may not be the best, but they're not going to change, so you get on with it. We practise under the lights. It's all new to most of our players. We're only learning about these fifty-over matches. New Zealand's Stephen Fleming, at 23 years of age, has played almost sixty one-day internationals. Mike Atherton has played fifty. Someone like Gavin Larsen, in the New Zealand side, has played eighty or ninety. Last season in the Benson and Hedges Cup was the first time that we played the one-day international regulations in any of our domestic competitions. I did some calculations at the start of these games. We had a total of 296 one-day international appearances between us. New Zealand had 602. They're more accustomed to the angles, the strategic positions within the fielding restrictions. So we're learning, and to have got two up against what I think is a crack one-day team in their own country with their own spectators is a good effort. The grounds are packed, the music's going; we need to be strong and we are.

We're good box-office. It's a real roller-coaster ride watching England. We're up and then we're down.

JA

In fact, it is a thoroughly enjoyable match played in front of a packed house. Young continues his rich form, scoring 53 before, yet again, chucking his wicket away, and with contributions from Astle (34), Parore (24) and Doull a belligerent 23, New Zealand finish with 237. White claims 4 for 37.

DL

They should have got more on that pitch and it's not the biggest ground from side to side, though it's adequate in all other areas. It turns out to be one of those chases where you're always a bit behind, though it's always in your sights.

JA

England get to 67 without loss, and with no alarm. Knight is caught and bowled by Allott for 39 and, suddenly in the twilight, Chris Harris, the medium-paced swing bowler, bowls Atherton for 23 with a big in-swinging yorker. This is followed, in his next over, by Stewart and then by Hussain for 13. Harris has taken 3 for 12 off 32 balls and when Irani skies Larsen to mid-off, England are 127 for 5.

Thorpe and White put on 47, but with 64 still needed from nine overs Thorpe is caught behind off Doull for 55. Cork's bowling might have gone dramatically off the boil, but he has batted very sensibly on this trip and now he and White, both scampering between the wickets, take England to the verge of victory. Six runs are needed off the last three balls, bowled by Allott in his first one-day international, when White is run out for 39.

DL

They've all chipped in and got starts except Ronnie Irani, and that stand between Cork and White has got us up there. It's been power play from the pair of them. Given the situation they've kept their nerve.

Now Croft comes in. He plays one of those 'I don't care where it goes' shots and it hits the middle of the bat and goes to mid-wicket. Four. Now we're winning this. We need two off two balls. Croft opts to move away to leg and get the ball over the off side and this time Geoff Allott keeps his nerve. He bowls a full-length stump ball on the basis that if Croft misses it, I hit. Croft does miss it. Bowled for four.

Now we've got Darren Gough going in. 'I'm the man.' He goes out there with us needing one to tie, two to win. He's got his fresh-air bat with him and he's got one ball from Allott to face.

JA

Gough heaves, massively, and misses but Cork has already decided to run to the wicket-keeper and the bye ties the match. I feel rather sorry for my colleague from Radio New Zealand, who is commentating from square leg through a smoked-glass window at the time and appears to lose sight of that crucial final ball completely.

DL

It's been great for anybody watching. We're slightly disappointed with the tie. We could have wrapped it up here. Just a run here or there. A little misfield, perhaps. But it's been great entertainment. And after three matches we're undefeated.

We may be disappointed, but they're absolutely flat in the New Zealand dressing room. They can't win the series now. I go in there afterwards and you could hear a pin drop. There's not a word being spoken.

After games like that the players rest the next day. That's my decision and I stand by it. They get away and they come up for it when it matters for the next match. I always give them a day off to recharge. And they need it. I don't count travel days as a day off. We might plan the next game on the evening of that day off, and if it's a game under lights we might go to the ground while the lights are on and just do a fielding session. Though the next game is a day-match in Auckland, where the weather is still dodgy, with the result that the Saturday game is put off to Sunday.

JA

Blackwater rafting is on the Agnews' itinerary as we make our way back to Auckland for the fourth one-day international. Again, there are a couple of days to kill and, rather than doing the journey in less than an hour by flying with the team, we spend one afternoon underground with our bottoms stuck in rubber tyres, bouncing our way down rivers and through caves which are lit, rather eerily, by glow-worms. A most interesting experience, which is more than can be said for the match which follows. Put simply, it is a shocker. It is now very difficult to tell which team is playing the worse cricket.

England bring in Silverwood for Cork in a match which is reduced by a damp start to 43 overs per side. New Zealand reach 113 for 2 and then collapse, failing even to last the distance as they are bowled out in the fortieth over for 153.

England's reply begins dramatically with Knight punching his first delivery from Davis and breaking his index finger in three places. Atherton makes 9, Thorpe 7, Hussain 3, Irani 0, and when Stewart, the top scorer, falls for 42 England are 91 for 5, with 63 runs required to win the series from thirteen overs. White scores a fluent 32 before driving Harris to extra cover and, as the countdown begins, Croft is run out for 20 with 22 required from 23 balls. Gough drives the next delivery back to Larsen and is caught and bowled, and when Caddick is bowled by Larsen first ball we all assume that Silverwood, the non-striker, will walk off the ground. Surely Knight is not going to bat, is he?

Sure enough, Knight emerges from the England dressing room, his right hand heavily bandaged. We have already been told that he needs immediate surgery – and to add to Knight's courage, he knows that he has one ball to face in this over. Holding his bat with one hand, he survives, and it is now up to Silverwood to score the remaining 21 runs from eighteen deliveries.

How has such a terrible match produced this thrilling

183

climax? My mobile telephone rings. It is ABC Radio in Sydney. They want me to commentate on the last couple of overs for them. So I stand outside the commentary box, with the telephone pinned to my ear and watch, agog, as Silverwood does all he can not only to win the match, but to keep Knight away from the strike. This he achieves, but in going for one big hit too many the youngster is eventually caught at long-off for 12 to give New Zealand victory by 9 runs and bring them back into the series. As I finish my stint on the ABC, the loudspeaker beside me begins to blast out more pop music. 'Don't, whatever you do, resort to this in Australia,' I plead, as I close my commentary.

'Don't worry, Aggers,' comes the reply from the presenter. 'We've tried it already!'

DL

People are reporting that we're just wanting to go home. That's absolute garbage. We're here to win cricket matches. We are professionals and that's what we're here to do. You can't win. If somebody asks you the question in an interview, 'Are you looking forward to going home?' I reply, 'Yes, we are. It'll be nice to get back. But we've got a game to play.' That last bit always gets knocked off and the line is, 'They want to go home.' It's just not the way it is. And you're powerless.

JA

It is extremely disappointing to watch England's cricket deteriorate so quickly. They have not had one proper practice since the one-day series began, and it shows. The bowling is rusty; 35 wides have been bowled in the four matches so far and while I do not blame the players for wanting to get home after such a long tour on which wives and families have been effectively banned, the disappointment I feel is that they should be winning every game they can. England have lacked consistency for years and now, confronted by a team which, frankly, several county sides

184

should beat without too much difficulty, they seem to be missing the chance to build a winning roll which, hopefully, would start them off well in the summer. It would be terrific, especially bearing in mind the poor start to this tour, if it ended on a high note. I fancy, though, that it is now too late to halt the slide.

A further fourteen wides are bowled in Wellington as New Zealand bat first in the match which will decide the series. That is a final tally of 49 wides bowled by England in the series. Astle scores 94 from 129 balls, but apart from Harris, who chimes in with 36, he receives no support and New Zealand's total of 228 looks to be a good twenty runs below par.

In fact, it proves to be comfortable enough to ensure that New Zealand win the match and square the series. Atherton makes 43, having been bowled by a no-ball in the first over, and Thorpe is dropped twice on his way to the top score, 55. At 107 for 3 in the twenty-eighth over England are well placed, needing 122 more at less than 6 runs per over. So why is Silverwood, number 11 the previous match, shoved up the order to number 5 ahead of Crawley? It certainly suggests to the spectators that England are panicking and when, after scoring 4 from 8 balls, Silverwood heaves horribly across the line and is bowled by Patel, that feeling appears to spread to the England dressing room.

Crawley is leg-before to Larsen for 11. Russell, playing in his first match for weeks, scores 2 and White 0, to leave England hopelessly out of contention. New Zealand win by 28 runs, and while the players shake hands beneath us at the end of another tour, their anticipation at returning home must be tinged with some dissatisfaction at the way it has finished.

DL

We really should have won one of those last two games. It's very disappointing, but we have been playing static cricket, though I reckon the team was certainly up for them. We played non-inventive cricket and we got what we deserved.

People are just starting to let me know, as we're ready to come home, that I have borne the brunt of the attacks in the press, so I have a clear-the-air meeting with them. I just ask them why. 'I don't mind criticism of the team, criticism of the tactics, criticism of the way we bat, bowl, field, but I don't know why you get into this ridicule. I can't get my head round that and why you have to be just taking the mickey all the time. There's no need for it. You just make me out to look an idiot and I'm not.' Other managers have had their heads made into potatoes or turnips. Mine's been done as a sheep. What sort of journalism is that?

At the end of it all, the match referee, Peter Burge, tells me that our team was excellent and it's been the easiest series he's had to deal with. New Zealand Cricket's chief executive, Christopher Doig, says, 'The lads have been an absolute credit to you.' Glenn Turner says, 'This is a very good England team just waiting to happen.' So you take all that on board.

It makes it all the more frustrating that we are portrayed in the way we are by the press. We can't do anything about it. We've won in New Zealand in the Tests 2-nil. We've scored 300 to win in the fourth innings, which hasn't been done since the 1920s. We've squared a one-day series with a team perhaps not suited to one-day cricket against a crack side.

Meanwhile our Under-19s have been to Pakistan and won there. Our 'A' Team has been to Australia and won there. From my point of view, in the job that I do, I think we're really making progress. We should be shouting that from the rooftops, and when it gets negative that's when you're absolutely powerless and you sit back and think that it's just 'Let's knock the England cricket team'.

I just wish we could be seen in a more positive light. That's the frustration of the job which you have no control over, so you just get on with it. It will be seen that I have a difficult time with the press. The majority of those lads are fine. They're good company and smashing people. But if one or two of them, because of their line of work, have to dag, I've no control over that.

POSTSCRIPT

PETER BAXTER
As I pack my briefcase up in Broadcasting House and
prepare for another drive home in the grey light of dawn it
seems a very long time since I walked across the apron at
Harare airport to start, with England, their winter tour.
Every tour is locked away as a file in the memory bank of
experience, some so vivid it is incredible to think that they
were a decade or more ago. Even the night shifts in the
studio, keeping in touch with Aggers and nowadays, all too
often, fighting for space on the airwaves, command a few
megabites of memory.

What will I remember from this winter? Well, we were as
tense in Studio 3H as any in Lancaster Park, Christchurch, as
Cork and Crawley clawed their way to what was a remarkable win. I found myself wondering whether the team
would have had the necessary self-confidence to get those
305 runs if that match had come before the restorative win in
Wellington. What a difference success makes. With one more
run in the Bulawayo Test, might the one-day series that
followed have had a different outcome? Certainly the excitement of Henry Blofeld on that dramatic last afternoon in
Bulawayo will remain with me.

A press attaché will travel with the England team on their
next tour. Will that make a difference? Or will the first story
reckoned by the team to be negative put matters right back
where they started? We all (and journalists and broadcasters

are worse than sportsmen at this) tend to react badly to criticism. I know that one bad letter outweighs ten nice ones. As far as sportsmen are concerned, the magic formula is winning. There are some tough battles ahead for England, though.

Already, during my last few nights in Broadcasting House, I have been taking the opportunity of having a word with my opposite number in the Australian Broadcasting Corporation, Alan Marks, to discuss broadcasting arrangements for the summer's Ashes series. As I drive home my mind is already thinking of how England will tackle that large obstacle. The bandwagon never stops rolling and I know that 'Bumble', as he boards the homeward-bound jumbo, will be thinking ahead, too.

DAVID LLOYD

Australia are rated the best team in the world. The challenge is there for us. We're going to be second favourites. We're going to need to be on the very top of our game. But we do have a nucleus of players.

I think that we have achieved something on this tour. Zimbabwe was frustrating because of the two drawn Test Matches. That's not a series, it's two Test Matches. And I know that we were the better side. But we didn't win. We played poorly. That's my job. I hold my hands up and admit it, and my team was left in no doubt that we played poorly and the challenge was to get hold of it and turn it round in New Zealand, which we did.

People will remember our trip to Zimbabwe for having lost the one-day internationals three-nil. India went just afterwards for a one-day international and got beaten comprehensively. Zimbabwe are a difficult team to beat in one-day cricket in their own country.

India beat South Africa in India and then got a good hiding in South Africa. We beat New Zealand in back-to-back Test Matches in New Zealand. They've since beaten Sri Lanka in back-to-back Test Matches in New Zealand.

189

If Australia are the best side in the world at the moment, I think Pakistan probably run them quite close. In my mind, West Indies, South Africa, England and India are the next pack and I wouldn't separate them. We're striving to get into that top three and we've no better test than this Ashes series. We'll have respect for the team that we play, but we won't be frightened of them.

For everything that's gone on, though, we've had a terrific tour. It's been excellent. I've got the best job in the world: the coach to the England cricket team. There are ups and downs and I accept that, and I do react and I'll have to learn not to react, but at fifty I don't give myself much of a chance of that. I've got a grand bunch of lads. I'm willing them to do well all the time and sometimes you've got to lay the law down, but it's a case of encouragement, support, trust and confidence. That's what my job revolves round and I wouldn't change it for the world.

I go back to the *Daily Telegraph* cutting by Christopher Martin-Jenkins that I carry around with me. Our lads are fed up of hearing it. We're looking to do what Australia are doing and that's winning Test Matches in all sorts of conditions. And we'll do that with 'sharply honed, dedicated and committed players, an aggressive approach, attacking bowling with a cutting edge, superlative fielding, flexible, orthodox batting, with an emphasis on the psychological and the physical'. And the message there is that you must at this level be tough and ruthless. If there's any message that I want to get across, that's it.

Appendix I
SCORES AND RESULTS

Zimbabwe

30 November 1996   v. Zimbabwe Country districts, at Harare South
Country districts: 198–9 (45.3 overs) (G. Whittall
     58; G. Rennie 32; Mullaly 3–35; Irani 3–46)
Match abandoned (rain)

1 December   v. ZCU President's XI at Harare Sports Club
England: 211–5 (50 overs) (Stewart 105; Hussain
     50; Brandes 3–42)
President's XI: 215–5 (45.5 overs) (Erasmus 67;
     Campbell 45; G. Whittall 36 n.o.)
President's XI won by 5 wickets

3–6 December   v. Mashonaland, at Harare Sports Club
England: 197 (Croft 80 n.o.; Thorpe 35; Kirtley 5–53)
     and 180 (Crawley 74; Hussain 39; Brent 4–22;
     P. Strang 4–56)
Mashonaland: 280 (Houghton 110; Campbell 55;
     Wishart 45; Tufnell 5–78; Croft 4–65) and 98–3
     (Campbell 53 n.o.; Houghton 34)
Mashonaland won by 7 wickets

8 December   v. Matabeleland, at Bulawayo Athletic Club
England: 210–9 (50 overs) (Knight 58; Crawley 30;
     G. Whittall 4–45; A. Whittall 3–35)
Matabeleland: 151 (43.3 overs) (G. Whittall 35;
     James 33; Abrams 33; Croft 3–42)
England won by 59 runs

191

10–13 December   v. Matabeleland, at Bulawayo Athletic Club
England: 334 (Knight 114; Crawley 63; Stewart 39;
Hussain 38; Streak 3–65) and 230–5 dec. (Thorpe
65; Atherton 55; Stewart 43; Hussain 40;
Vaghmaria 3–58)
Matabeleland: 188 (James 62; Gough 6–64) and 261
(Dekker 104; Streak 67; J. Rennie 30 n.o.; Gough
5–75; Croft 4–65)
England won by 115 runs

FIRST ONE-DAY INTERNATIONAL
at Queen's Club, Bulawayo
15 December
Toss: Zimbabwe

ENGLAND
Knight lbw b Streak	13	(28–1)	(7th)
Stewart[†] c A. Flower b Streak	26	(41–2)	(11th)
Atherton* c sub. (A. Whittall) b G. Flower	23	(96–4)	(31st)
Thorpe b Brandes	1	(47–3)	(14th)
Hussain not out	49		
Crawley c Campbell b Rennie	10	(125–5)	(38th)
Irani c and b Rennie	7	(134–6)	(40th)
Mullally c and b Rennie	0	(134–7)	(40th)
Croft c G. Flower b Streak	0	(135–8)	(41st)
Gough run out	9	(150–9)	(44th)
Silverwood c Houghton b Strang	1		(46th)
Extras (lb 6; w 3; nb 4)	13		
Total	152	(45.5 overs)	

BOWLING	Overs	Mdns	Runs	Wkts
Brandes	8	2	28	1
J. Rennie	8	1	27	3
Streak	9	1	30	3
G. Whittall	5	0	17	0
P. Strang	9.4	1	27	1
G. Flower	6	0	17	1

* Captain; † wicket-keeper

192

ZIMBABWE

G. Flower b Silverwood	14	(33–1)	(9th)
Waller run out	48	(97–5)	(29th)
A. Flower[†] c Knight b Silverwood	10	(58–2)	(18th)
Houghton c Crawley b Gough	2	(73–3)	(21st)
Evans c Stewart b Gough	1	(87–4)	(25th)
G. Whittall c Stewart b Mullally	13	(106–6)	(32nd)
Campbell* not out	32		
P. Strang c Stewart b Mullally	0	(106–7)	(32nd)
Streak c and b Croft	11	(137–8)	(41st)
Brandes not out	8		
J. Rennie did not bat			
Extras (lb 9; w 4; nb 1)	14		
Total	153 for 8 (43.5 overs)		

BOWLING	Overs	Mdns	Runs	Wkts
Mullally	10	2	24	2
Gough	10	2	31	2
Silverwood	10	0	27	2
Croft	5	0	32	1
Irani	6.5	1	25	0
Thorpe	2	1	5	0

Umpires: Russell Tiffin, Quentin Goosen

Zimbabwe won by 2 wickets (6.1 overs to spare)
Man of the Match: Alistair Campbell

FIRST TEST MATCH
at Queen's Club, Bulawayo
Toss: Zimbabwe

ZIMBABWE First Innings		Second Innings	
G. Flower c Hussain b Silverwood .	43	lbw b Gough	0
Carlisle c Crawley b Gough	0	c Atherton b Mullally ..	4
Campbell* c Silverwood b Croft ...	84	b Croft	29
Houghton c Stewart b Croft	34	c Croft b Tufnell	37
A. Flower† c Stewart b Tufnell	112	c Crawley b Tufnell	14
Waller c Crawley b Croft	15	c Knight b Gough	50
G. Whittall c Atherton b Silverwood	7	(8) c Croft b Tufnell	56
P. Strang c Tufnell b Silverwood ...	38	(9) c Crawley b Croft ...	19
Streak b Mullally	19	(10) not out	8
B. Strang not out	4	(7) c Mullally b Tufnell ..	3
Olonga c Knight b Tufnell	0	c Stewart b Silverwood .	0
Extras (lb 4; w 3; nb 13)	20	(b 4; lb 6; w 2; nb 2)	14
Total	376	234	

Fall of wickets: 1st inns. 1–3 (Carlisle); 2–130 (G. Flower); 3–136 (Campbell); 4–206 (Houghton); 5–235 (Waller); 6–252 (Whittall); 7–331 (P. Strang); 8–372 (Streak); 9–376 (A. Flower)

2nd inns. 1–6 (Carlisle); 2–6 (G. Flower); 3–57 (Campbell); 4–82 (A. Flower); 5–103 (Houghton); 6–111 (B. Strang); 7–178 (Waller); 8–209 (P. Strang); 9–233 (G. Whittall)

BOWLING	Overs	Mdns	Runs	Wkts	Overs	Mdns	Runs	Wkts
Mullally	23	4	69	1	18	5	49	1
Gough	26	4	87	1	12	2	44	2
Silverwood	18	5	63	3	7	3	8	1
Croft	44	15	77	3	33	9	62	2
Tufnell	26.5	4	76	2	31	12	61	4

ENGLAND   First Innings

		Second Innings	
Knight lbw b Olonga	56	run out	96
Atherton* lbw b P. Strang	16	b Olonga	4
Stewart† lbw b P. Strang	48	c Campbell b P. Strang	73
Hussain c B. Strang b Streak	113	c Carlisle b P. Strang	0
Thorpe c Campbell b P. Strang	13	(6) c Campbell b Streak	2
Crawley c A. Flower b P. Strang	112	(5) c Carlisle b Whittall	7
Croft lbw b Olonga	7		
Gough c G. Flower b Olonga	2	(7) not out	3
Silverwood c Houghton b P. Strang	0		
Mullally c Waller b Streak	4		
Tufnell not out	2		
Extras (b 4; lb 4; w 1; nb 24)	33	(b 2; lb 13; w 3; nb 1)	19
Total	406	(for 6 wkts)	204

Fall of wickets: 1st inns. 1–48 (Atherton); 2–92 (Knight); 3–160 (Stewart); 4–180 (Thorpe); 5–328 (Hussain); 6–340 (Croft); 7–344 (Gough); 8–353 (Silverwood); 9–378 (Mullally)

2nd inns: 1–17 (Atherton); 2–154 (Stewart); 3–156 (Hussain); 4–178 (Crawley); 5–182 (Thorpe); 6–204 (Knight)

BOWLING	Overs	Mdns	Runs	Wkts	Overs	Mdns	Runs	Wkts
Streak	36	8	86	2	11	0	64	1
B. Strang	17	5	54	0				
P. Strang	58.4	14	123	5	14	0	63	2
Olonga	23	2	90	3	2	0	16	1
G. Whittall	10	2	25	0	2	0	10	1
G. Flower	7	3	20	0	8	0	36	0

Umpires: Steve Dunne (New Zealand), Ian Robinson (Zimbabwe)

Match drawn (with scores level)

Man of the Match: Nick Knight

Brian Johnston/Veuve Clicquot Champagne Moment: Nick Knight (for his last-over 6)

SECOND TEST MATCH
at Harare Sports Club
26–30 December
Toss: Zimbabwe

ENGLAND	First Innings		Second Innings	
Knight c A. Flower b Olonga		15	c Campbell b Strang	30
Atherton* c Campbell b Whittall		13	c Campbell b Streak	1
Stewart† c G. Flower b Streak		19	not out	101
Hussain c A. Flower b Streak		11	c Houghton b Strang	6
Thorpe c Dekker b Streak		5	not out	50
Crawley not out		47		
White c Campbell b Whittall		9		
Croft c G. Flower b Whittall		14		
Gough b Strang		2		
Mullally c and b Whittall		0		
Tufnell b Streak		9		
Extras (b1; lb 5; w 1; nb 5)		12	(lb 5; nb 2))	7
Total		156	(for 3 wkts)	195

Fall of wickets: 1st inns. 1–24 (Knight); 2–50 (Atherton); 3–50 (Stewart); 4–65 (Thorpe); 5–73 (Hussain); 6–94 (White); 7–128 (Croft); 8–133 (Gough); 9–134 (Mullally)
2nd inns. 1–7 (Atherton); 2–75 (Knight); 3–89 (Hussain)

BOWLING	Overs	Mdns	Runs	Wkts	Overs	Mdns	Runs	Wkts
Streak	24.1	7	43	4	18	5	47	1
Brandes	16	6	35	0	21	6	45	0
Olonga	9	1	23	1	7	0	31	0
Whittall	16	5	18	4	14	6	16	0
Strang	18	7	31	1	26	6	42	2
G. Flower					7	2	9	0

ZIMBABWE   First Innings

G. Flower c Crawley b Gough	73
Dekker c Stewart b Mullally	2
Campbell* c Thorpe b White	22
Houghton c Stewart b Gough	29
A. Flower[†] lbw b Gough	6
Waller lbw b Tufnell	4
G. Whittall b Gough	1
P. Strang not out	47
Streak c Crawley b Croft	7
Brandes c Gough b Croft	9
Olonga c Hussain b Croft	0
Extras (lb 8; w 1; nb 6)	15
Total	215

Fall of wickets: 1st inns. 1–5 (Dekker); 2–46 (Campbell); 3–110 (Houghton); 4–130 (A. Flower); 5–136 (Waller); 6–138 (Whittall); 7–159 (G. Flower); 8–197 (Streak); 9–211 (Brandes)

BOWLING	Overs	Mdns	Runs	Wkts
Mullally	23	7	32	1
Gough	26	10	40	4
Croft	15	2	39	3
White	16	4	41	1
Tufnell	25	3	55	1

Umpires: K.T. Francis (Sri Lanka), Russell Tiffin (Zimbabwe)

Match drawn
Man of the Match: Grant Flower
Brian Johnston/Veuve Clicquot Champagne Moment: Alec Stewart (for his two fours off Olonga to reach his hundred)

SECOND ONE-DAY INTERNATIONAL
at Harare Sports Club
1 January 1997
Toss: England

ZIMBABWE

G. Flower c Hussain b Gough		4	(14–2) (4th)
Waller b Mullally		0	(2–1) (1st)
Campbell* c Stewart b Gough		14	(38–4) (10th)
Houghton c Croft b Mullally		5	(26–3) (7th)
A. Flower† c Stewart b Mullally		63	(200–8) (48th)
Evans lbw b Croft		32	(97–5) (23rd)
G. Whittall run out		14	(125–6) (32nd)
P. Strang c Atherton b Croft		1	(126–7) (33rd)
Streak not out		43	
Brandes c Atherton b Gough		0	(200–9) (49th)
J. Rennie b Gough		0	(49th)
Extras (lb 11; w 10; nb 3)		24	
Total		200	(48.5 overs)

BOWLING	Overs	Mdns	Runs	Wkts
Mullally	9	1	29	3
Gough	8.5	1	43	4
Silverwood	6	0	30	0
White	10	1	39	0
Croft	10	2	33	2
Irani	5	0	15	0

ENGLAND

Knight c Houghton b Brandes		0	(1–1) (3rd)
Stewart† c A. Flower b Whittall		41	(67–2) (13th)
Crawley st A. Flower b Strang		73	(157–5) (38th)
Hussain lbw b Whittall		7	(95–3) (23rd)
Atherton* c Whittall b Strang		25	(137–4) (34th)
Irani st A. Flower b Strang		5	(165–6) (40th)
White lbw b Streak		4	(169–7) (41st)
Croft not out		10	
Gough not out		2	
Extras (b 2; lb 5; w 5)		12	
Total (for 7 wkts)		179	(42 overs)

Did not bat: Mullally, Silverwood.

BOWLING	Overs	Mdns	Runs	Wkts
Brandes	6	2	25	1
Rennie	5	0	26	0
Streak	8	0	41	1
Whittall	8	0	30	2
Evans	2	0	6	0
Strang	9	0	24	3
G. Flower	4	0	20	0

Umpires: Ian Robinson, Graham Evans

Zimbabwe won by 6 runs on a revised target (185 in 42 overs)
Men of the Match: Crawley/Strang

THIRD ONE-DAY INTERNATIONAL
at Harare Sports Club
3 January
Toss: England

ZIMBABWE

G. Flower c Mullally b White	62	(131–2)	(29th)
Waller run out	19	(58–1)	(15th)
Campbell* not out	80		
A. Flower† c Stewart b Irani	35	(181–3)	(38th)
Evans c Stewart b Gough	1	(183–4)	(40th)
G. Whittall b Croft	1	(190–5)	(41st)
Houghton c Stewart b Mullally	19	(220–6)	(47th)
P. Strang run out	13	(249–7)	(50th)
Extras (b 4; lb 5; w 8; nb 2)	19		
Total (for 7 wkts)	249	(50 overs)	

Did not bat: Brandes, Streak, Rennie.

BOWLING	Overs	Mdns	Runs	Wkts
Mullally	10	3	39	1
Gough	10	1	42	1
Silverwood	5	0	27	0
White	7	0	39	1
Irani	10	0	39	2
Croft	8	0	54	1

ENGLAND

Knight c A. Flower b Brandes	3	(9–1)	(3rd)
Stewart† c A. Flower b Brandes	29	(45–4)	(15th)
Crawley lbw b Brandes	0	(13–2)	(5th)
Hussain c A. Flower b Brandes	0	(13–3)	(5th)
Atherton* c A. Flower b Brandes	18	(54–5)	(17th)
Irani c Whittall b Streak	0	(55–6)	(18th)
White c A. Flower b Streak	0	(63–7)	(20th)
Croft not out	30		
Gough c Streak b Strang	7	(77–8)	(23rd)
Mullally b Whittall	20	(118–9)	(30th)
Silverwood c Evans b Whittall	0		
Extras (w 8; nb 3)	11		
Total	118	(30 overs)	

BOWLING	Overs	Mdns	Runs	Wkts
Brandes	10	0	28	5
Rennie	3	0	11	0
Streak	10	0	50	2
Strang	5	0	18	1
Whittall	2	0	11	2

Umpires: Ian Robinson, Russell Tiffin

Zimbabwe won by 131 runs
Man of the Match: Eddo Brandes

Zimbabwe won one-day series 3–0

New Zealand

10 January 1997   v. New Zealand Academy XI, at New Plymouth
NZ Academy: 201 (40.1 overs) (McMillan 58;
    Loveridge 54; Caddick 3–44)
Match abandoned: rain

13–16 January   v. New Zealand Select XI, at Palmerston North
Select XI: 138 (Spearman 41; White 4–15) and 176
    (Pocock 43; Tufnell 5–58; Silverwood 3–29)
England: 427–8 dec. (Stewart 153 n.o.; Hussain
    139; Knight 46; Crawley 35; Morrison 4–81)
England won by an innings and 113 runs

18–21 January   v. Northern Districts, at Hamilton
Northern Districts: 69 (White 3–17; Cork 3–18;
    Gough 3–23) and 259 (Pocock 69; Parlane 74;
    Mullally 4–52; Gough 3–51)
England: 294 (Thorpe 71; Crawley 65; Stewart 40;
    Knight 39; Tait 5–96; Styris 4–110) and 38–0
England won by 10 wickets

FIRST TEST MATCH
at Eden Park, Auckland
24–28 January
Toss: England

NEW ZEALAND First Innings		Second Innings	
Young lbw b Mullally	44	(2) c Hussain b Cork ..	3
Pocock lbw b Gough	70	(1) lbw b Gough	20
Parore c Stewart b Cork	6	st Stewart b Tufnell ...	33
Fleming c and b Cork	129	c Crawley b Tufnell ...	9
Astle c Stewart b White	10	(6) not out	102
Vaughan lbw b Cork	3	(7) lbw b Tufnell	2
Cairns c Stewart b White	67	(8) b Mullally	7
Germon*† c Stewart b Gough	14	(5) run out	13
Patel lbw b Gough	0	lbw b Mullally	0
Doull c Knight b Gough	5	b Gough	26
Morrison not out	6	not out	14
Extras (b 5; lb 12; nb 17; w 2)	36	(lb 11; nb 8)	19
Total	390	(for 9 wkts)	248

Fall of wickets: 1st inns. 1–85 (Young); 2–114 (Parore); 3–193 (Pocock);
 4–210 (Astle); 5–215 (Vaughan); 6–333 (Cairns); 7–362 (Germon);
 8–362 (Patel); 9–380 (Doull)
2nd inns. 1–17 (Young); 2–28 (Pocock); 3–47 (Fleming); 4–88 (Germon);
 5–90 (Parore); 6–92 (Vaughan); 7–101 (Cairns); 8–105 (Patel); 9–142
 (Doull)

BOWLING	Overs	Mdns	Runs	Wkts	Overs	Mdns	Runs	Wkts
Cork	32.5	8	96	3	16	3	45	1
Mullally	27	11	55	1	26	10	47	2
Gough	32	6	91	4	22	2	66	2
Tufnell	25	5	80	0	40	18	53	3
White	15	3	51	2	10	2	26	0

APPENDIX I

ENGLAND   First Innings

Knight lbw b Doull	5
Atherton* c and b Patel	83
Stewart† c and b Doull	173
Hussain c Fleming b Patel	8
Thorpe hit wkt b Cairns	119
Crawley run out	14
White lbw b Vaughan	0
Cork c Young b Morrison	59
Gough c Germon b Morrison	2
Mullally c Germon b Morrison	21
Tufnell not out	19
Extras (b 2; lb 12; nb 2; w 2)	18
Total	521

Fall of wickets: 1–18 (Knight); 2–200 (Atherton); 3–222 (Hussain); 4–304 (Stewart); 5–339 (Crawley); 6–339 (White); 7–453 (Thorpe); 8–471 (Gough); 9–478 (Cork)

BOWLING	Overs	Mdns	Runs	Wkts
Morrison	24.4	4	104	3
Doull	39	10	118	2
Cairns	30	3	103	1
Astle	14	3	33	0
Vaughan	36	10	57	1
Patel	44	8	92	2

Umpires: Steve Bucknor (West Indies), Steve Dunne (New Zealand)

Match drawn
Men of the Match: Astle, Stewart
Brian Johnston/Veuve Clicquot Champagne Moment: Nathan Astle (for the four to make his hundred off the last ball of the match)

30 January–2 February v. New Zealand 'A', at Wanganui
> New Zealand 'A': 181 (Horne 64; Murray 49;
> Silverwood 6–44) and 288 (Harris 71; Howell
> 66; Spearman 47; Caddick 3–52)
> England: 107 (Irani 40; Davis 4–22; Allott 4–44)
> and 272 (Russell 61 n.o.; Hussain 57; Croft
> 49; Allott 4–76)
> New Zealand 'A' won by 90 runs

SECOND TEST MATCH
at Basin Reserve, Wellington
6–10 February
Toss: New Zealand

NEW ZEALAND First Innings		Second Innings	
Young c Stewart b Gough	8	(2) c Stewart b Tufnell	64
Pocock c Cork b Caddick	6	(1) c Knight b Gough	56
Parore c Stewart b Gough	4	lbw b Croft	15
Fleming c and b Caddick	1	c and b Croft	0
Astle c Croft b Gough	36	(7) c Stewart b Gough	4
Cairns c Hussain b Gough	3	(8) c Knight b Caddick	22
Germon*† c Stewart b Caddick	10	(6) b Gough	11
Patel c Cork b Caddick	45	(5) lbw b Croft	0
Doull c Stewart b Gough	0	c Knight b Gough	0
Allott c Knight b Cork	1	b Caddick	2
Vettori not out	3	not out	2
Extras (lb 5; nb 2)	7	(b 5; lb 4; nb 6)	15
Total	124		191

Fall of wickets: 1st inns. 1–14 (Pocock); 2–18 (Young); 3–19 (Parore); 4–19
(Fleming); 5–23 (Cairns); 6–48 (Germon); 7–85 (Astle); 8–85 (Doull);
9–106 (Allott)
2nd inns. 1–89 (Young); 2–125 (Parore); 3–125 (Fleming); 4–125 (Patel);
5–161 (Germon); 6–164 (Pocock); 7–175 (Astle); 8–175 (Doull); 9–182
(Allott)

BOWLING	Overs	Mdns	Runs	Wkts	Overs	Mdns	Runs	Wkts
Cork	14	4	34	1	10	1	42	0
Caddick	18.3	5	45	4	27.2	11	40	2
Gough	16	6	40	5	23	9	52	4
Croft					20	9	19	3
Tufnell					23	9	29	1

APPENDIX I

First Innings
Knight c Patel b Doull   8
Atherton* lbw b Doull   30
Stewart[†] c Fleming b Allott   52
Hussain c Young b Vettori   64
Thorpe st Germon b Patel 108
Crawley c Germon b Doull   56
Cork lbw b Astle   7
Croft c Fleming b Doull   0
Gough c Fleming b Doull   18
Caddick c Allott b Vettori   20
Tufnell not out   6
   Extras (b 3; lb 9; nb 2)   14

   Total 383

Fall of wickets: 1–10 (Knight); 2–80 (Atherton); 3–106 (Stewart); 4–213 (Hussain); 5–331 (Thorpe); 6–331 (Crawley); 7–331 (Croft); 8–357 (Cork); 9–357 (Gough)

BOWLING	Overs	Mdns	Runs	Wkts
Doull	28	10	75	5
Allott	31	6	91	1
Vettori	34.3	10	98	2
Cairns	4	2	8	0
Astle	14	5	30	1
Patel	24	6	59	1
Pocock	2	0	10	0

Umpires: Steve Bucknor (West Indies), Doug Cowie (New Zealand)

England won by an innings and 68 runs
Man of the Match: Graham Thorpe
Brian Johnston/Veuve Clicquot Champagne Moment: Alec Stewart (for his 2nd innings catch of Astle)

THIRD TEST MATCH
at Lancaster Park, Christchurch
14–18 February
Toss: England

NEW ZEALAND First Innings		Second Innings	
Young b Cork	11	(2) c Knight b Tufnell	49
Pocock c Atherton b Croft	22	(1) b Cork	0
Horne c Thorpe b Gough	42	(8) c Stewart b Caddick	13
Fleming* st Stewart b Croft	62	c Knight b Tufnell	11
Astle c Hussain b Croft	15	c Hussain b Croft	5
Parore† c Hussain b Croft	59	(3) c Stewart b Gough	8
Cairns c Stewart b Caddick	57	(6) c Knight b Tufnell	52
Doull run out	1	(7) c Knight b Croft	5
Vettori run out	25	not out	29
Davis c Hussain b Croft	8	b Gough	1
Allott not out	8	c Stewart b Gough	1
Extras (b 1; lb 16; nb 19)	36	(lb 8; nb 4)	12
Total	346		186

Fall of wickets: 1st inns. 1–14 (Young); 2–78 (Pocock); 3–106 (Horne);
4–137 (Astle); 5–201 (Fleming); 6–283 (Parore); 7–288 (Doull); 8–310
(Cairns); 9–338 (Vettori)
2nd inns. 1–0 (Pocock); 2–42 (Parore); 3–61 (Fleming); 4–76 (Astle); 5–80
(Young); 6–89 (Doull); 7–107 (Horne); 8–178 (Cairns); 9–184 (Davis)

BOWLING	Overs	Mdns	Runs	Wkts	Overs	Mdns	Runs	Wkts
Cork	20	3	78	1	6	2	5	1
Caddick	32	8	64	1	10	1	25	1
Gough	21	3	70	1	13.3	5	42	3
Croft	39.1	5	95	5	31	13	48	2
Tufnell	16	6	22	0	28	9	58	3
Thorpe	1	1	0	0				

APPENDIX I

First Innings

		Second Innings	
Knight c Fleming b Allott	14	c Davis b Vettori	29
Atherton* not out	94	c Parore b Astle	118
Stewart† c sub (Harris) b Allott	15	c Pocock b Vettori	17
Hussain c Parore b Cairns	12	(5) c Fleming b Vettori .	33
Thorpe b Astle	18	(6) c and b Vettori	2
Crawley c Parore b Allott	1	(7) not out	40
Cork c Parore b Davis	16	(8) not out	39
Croft c Davis b Astle	31		
Gough b Vettori	0		
Caddick c sub (Harris) b Allott	4	(4) c Fleming b Doull . .	15
Tufnell c Young b Doull	13		
Extras (lb 4; w 1; nb 5)	10	(b 2; lb 8; w 1; nb 3) . . .	14
Total	228	(for 6 wkts)	307

Fall of wickets: 1st inns. 1–20 (Knight); 2–40 (Stewart); 3–70 (Hussain);
4–103 (Thorpe); 5–104 (Crawley); 6–145 (Cork); 7–198 (Croft); 8–199
(Gough); 9–210 (Caddick)
2nd inns. 1–64 (Knight); 2–116 (Stewart); 3–146 (Caddick); 4–226
(Atherton); 5–226 (Hussain); 6–231 (Thorpe)

BOWLING	Overs	Mdns	Runs	Wkts	Overs	Mdns	Runs	Wkts
Allott	18	3	74	4	12.4	2	32	0
Doull	17.4	3	49	1	21	8	57	1
Davis	18	2	50	1	18	6	43	0
Vettori	12	4	13	1	57	18	97	4
Cairns	8	5	12	1	10	1	23	0
Astle	11	2	26	2	28	10	45	1

Umpires: Steve Dunne (New Zealand), Daryl Hair (Australia)

England won by 4 wickets
Man of the Match: Mike Atherton
Brian Johnston/Veuve Clicquot Champagne Moment: Phil Tufnell (for
his run-out of Doull in the first innings)

207

FIRST ONE-DAY INTERNATIONAL
at Lancaster Park, Christchurch
20 February (day/night)
Toss: New Zealand

NEW ZEALAND

Young c Thorpe b Mullally	14	(24–1)	(6th)
Astle c Thorpe b Tufnell	50	(87–2)	(20th)
Parore c and b Tufnell	26	(100–3)	(29th)
Fleming st Stewart b Tufnell	34	(148–5)	(38th)
Cairns c Mullally b Tufnell	15	(134–4)	(34th)
Harris not out	48		
Germon*† b Cork	19	(203–6)	(49th)
Patel not out	1		
Extras (b 1; lb 8; w 4; nb 2)	15		
	―		
Total (for 6 wkts)	222	(50 overs)	

Did not bat: Doull, Larsen, Davis

BOWLING	Overs	Mdns	Runs	Wkts
Cork	9	0	51	1
Mullally	5	2	21	1
Croft	10	1	41	0
Gough	10	0	46	0
Tufnell	10	1	22	4
Thorpe	6	0	32	0

ENGLAND

Knight c Germon b Doull	8	(28–2)	(7th)
Atherton* b Patel	19	(28–1)	(6th)
Stewart† c Astle b Davis	81	(205–4)	(43rd)
Thorpe b Davis	82	(198–3)	(41st)
Hussain not out	11		
Crawley b Doull	0	(207–5)	(44th)
Cork c Young b Davis	5	(218–6)	(49th)
Croft not out	8		
Extras (lb 6; w 6)	12		
	―		
Total (for 6 wkts)	226	(48.5 overs)	

Did not bat: Gough, Mullally, Tufnell

BOWLING	Overs	Mdns	Runs	Wkts
Doull	10	0	33	2
Patel	7	0	43	1
Astle	4	0	26	0
Cairns	4	0	25	0
Davis	8.5	0	44	3
Larsen	8	0	23	0
Harris	7	0	26	0

Umpires: Chris King, Dave Quested

England won by 4 wickets (7 balls to spare)
Man of the Match: Phil Tufnell

SECOND ONE-DAY INTERNATIONAL
at Eden Park, Auckland
23 February
Toss: New Zealand

NEW ZEALAND

Young c Stewart b Irani	46	(96–3) (20th)
Astle c Stewart b Mullally	4	(24–1) (4th)
Parore run out	2	(44–2) (8th)
Fleming c Caddick b Gough	42	(138–4) (30th)
Cairns run out	79	(219–7) (47th)
Harris c sub (White) b Caddick	14	(189–5) (42nd)
Germon*† b Caddick	1	(202–6) (44th)
Patel run out	24	(253–8) (50th)
Larsen not out	12	
Extras (lb 9; w 16; nb 4)	29	
Total (for 8 wkts)	253	(50 overs)

Did not bat: Doull, Davis

BOWLING	Overs	Mdns	Runs	Wkts
Cork	10	0	51	0
Mullally	7	0	36	1
Caddick	6	0	33	2
Gough	10	0	65	1
Irani	7	0	26	1
Croft	10	1	33	0

OUT OF THE ROUGH

Knight not out 84
Stewart† lbw b Davis 30 (86–1) (11th)
Cork c Young b Larsen 4 (91–2) (12th)
Irani c Astle b Doull 0 (92–3) (13th)
Thorpe c and b Doull 4 (100–4) (15th)
Hussain* not out 9
  Extras (w 3) 3

  Total (for 4 wkts) .... 134 (19.3 overs)

Did not bat: Crawley, Gough, Croft, Caddick, Mullally

BOWLING	Overs	Mdns	Runs	Wkts
Davis	6	1	39	1
Doull	5	0	39	2
Larsen	5	0	31	1
Harris	2	0	8	0
Astle	1.3	0	17	0

Umpires: Brent Bowden, Doug Cowie

England won by 6 wickets on a revised target (132 in 26 overs)
Man of the Match: Nick Knight

THIRD ONE-DAY INTERNATIONAL
at McLean Park, Napier
26 February (day/night)
Toss: New Zealand

NEW ZEALAND

Young b Caddick	53	(145–5)	(32nd)
Astle c Stewart b Gough	34	(50–1)	(9th)
Germon*† st Stewart b Croft	22	(103–2)	(21st)
Fleming run out	12	(125–3)	(25th)
Cairns c Cork b Caddick	11	(140–4)	(30th)
Parore c and b White	24	(191–7)	(42nd)
Harris c Stewart b White	19	(178–6)	(40th)
Larsen c Stewart b Gough	18	(233–8)	(49th)
Doull b White	23		
Davis b White	1	(234–9)	(50th)
Allott not out	1		
Extras (lb 11; w 4; nb 4)	19		
Total	237	(49.4 overs)	

BOWLING	Overs	Mdns	Runs	Wkts
Cork	9	1	41	0
Caddick	10	2	43	2
Gough	10	0	34	2
Irani	5	0	29	0
Croft	10	0	42	1
White	5.4	0	37	4

ENGLAND

Knight c and b Allott	39	(67–1)	(12th)
Atherton* b Harris	23	(82–2)	(18th)
Stewart† b Harris	17	(87–3)	(20th)
Thorpe c Germon b Doull	55	(174–6)	(40th)
Hussain b Harris	13	(114–4)	(28th)
Irani c Doull b Larsen	4	(127–5)	(31st)
White run out	39	(232–7)	(50th)
Cork not out	31		
Croft b Allott	4	(236–8)	(50th)
Gough not out	0		
Extras (b 2; lb 3; w 5; nb 2)	12		
Total (for 8 wkts)	237	(50 overs)	

Did not bat: Caddick

BOWLING	Overs	Mdns	Runs	Wkts
Doull	9	0	53	1
Allott	9	2	50	2
Davis	10	0	40	0
Harris	10	3	20	3
Larsen	10	0	50	1
Astle	2	0	19	0

Umpires: Dave Quested, Chris King

Match tied
Man of the Match: Chris Harris

FOURTH ONE-DAY INTERNATIONAL
at Eden Park, Auckland
Late start after rain: 43 overs a side
Toss: England

NEW ZEALAND

Young c and b White	16	(53–1)	(11th)
Astle c Stewart b Irani	51	(113–3)	(26th)
Germon*† lbw b Gough	0	(54–2)	(12th)
Fleming c Hussain b Croft	37	(120–5)	(29th)
Cairns run out	2	(116–4)	(27th)
Parore c Croft b Caddick	13	(136–8)	(35th)
Harris c Hussain b Croft	0	(120–6)	(29th)
Larsen run out	2	(129–7)	(32nd)
Doull not out	13		
Davis b Caddick	0	(141–9)	(37th)
Allott b Gough	3		
Extras (b 2; lb 3; w 11)	16		
Total	153 (39.5 overs)		

BOWLING	Overs	Mdns	Runs	Wkts
Caddick	8	1	29	2
Silverwood	5	0	20	0
Gough	5.5	0	29	2
White	5	0	21	1
Croft	9	1	26	2
Irani	7	0	23	1

ENGLAND

Knight not out (retired hurt at 1–0; returned at 133–9) 1
Atherton* c Harris b Allott 9   (22–1) (4th)
Stewart† b Astle 42   (91–5) (29th)
Thorpe c Parore b Allott 7   (32–2) (6th)
Hussain b Davis 3   (41–3) (9th)
Irani c Fleming b Davis 0   (41–4) (9th)
White c Parore b Harris 32 (113–6) (36th)
Croft run out 20 (132–7) (40th)
Gough c and b Larsen 5 (132–8) (40th)
Caddick b Larsen 0 (133–9) (40th)
Silverwood c Allott b Larsen 12
   Extras (lb 6; w 7) 13

   Total . . . . 144 (41.3 overs)

BOWLING	Overs	Mdns	Runs	Wkts
Davis	6	0	32	2
Allott	5	1	21	2
Doull	6	1	15	0
Larsen	8.3	0	20	3
Harris	9	0	26	1
Astle	7	1	24	1

Umpires: Steve Dunne, Doug Cowie

New Zealand won by 9 runs
Men of the Match: Nathan Astle, Gavin Larsen

FIFTH ONE-DAY INTERNATIONAL
at Basin Reserve, Wellington
4 March
Toss: New Zealand

NEW ZEALAND
Young c Russell b Caddick	11	(28–1)	(7th)
Astle c Atherton b Silverwood	94	(197–5)	(44th)
Fleming lbw b Croft	17	(84–2)	(18th)
Cairns c Russell b White	1	(87–3)	(19th)
Parore lbw b Caddick	18	(122–4)	(27th)
Harris c Stewart b Gough	36	(206–7)	(46th)
Germon*† lbw b Caddick	2	(200–6)	(45th)
Patel not out	16		
Larsen run out	0	(208–8)	(47th)
Davis not out	7		
Extras (lb 10; w 14; nb 2)	26		
Total (for 8 wkts)	228	(50 overs)	

Did not bat: Allott

BOWLING	Overs	Mdns	Runs	Wkts
Caddick	10	1	35	3
Silverwood	10	0	53	1
Gough	10	1	48	1
White	10	0	44	1
Croft	10	1	38	1

ENGLAND
Atherton* run out	43	(107–3)	(28th)
Stewart c Patel b Allott	18	(43–1)	(9th)
Hussain st Germon b Harris	20	(77–2)	(18th)
Thorpe st Germon b Larsen	55	(173–9)	(44th)
Silverwood b Patel	4	(118–4)	(31st)
Crawley lbw b Larsen	11	(136–5)	(36th)
Russell† c Germon b Astle	2	(139–6)	(37th)
White c Germon b Astle	0	(139–7)	(37th)
Croft run out	2	(158–8)	(41st)
Gough c Fleming b Davis	16		
Caddick not out	12		
Extras (lb 8; w 8; nb 1)	17		
Total	200	(47.5 overs)	

214

BOWLING	Overs	Mdns	Runs	Wkts
Allott	8	0	40	1
Davis	7.5	0	44	1
Larsen	10	0	31	2
Harris	10	2	22	1
Patel	7	0	29	1
Astle	5	0	26	2

Umpires: Steve Dunne, Evan Watkin

New Zealand won by 28 runs
Man of the Match: Nathan Astle

One-Day International series shared 2–2

Appendix II

England Test Averages

BATTING	M	Inns	N.O.	Runs	H.S.	Ave.	100s
A.J. Stewart	5	8	1	498	173	71.14	2
J.P. Crawley	5	7	2	277	112	55.40	1
M.A. Atherton	5	8	1	359	118	51.29	1
G.P. Thorpe	5	8	1	317	119	45.29	2
D.G. Cork	3	4	1	121	59	40.33	0
N.V. Knight	5	8	0	253	96	31.62	0
N. Hussain	5	8	0	247	113	30.87	1
P.C.R. Tufnell	5	5	3	49	19*	24.50	0
R.D.B Croft	4	4	0	52	14	13.00	0
A.R. Caddick	2	3	0	39	20	13.00	0
A.D. Mullally	3	3	0	25	21	8.33	0
D. Gough	5	6	1	27	18	5.40	0
C. White	2	2	0	9	9	4.50	0
C.E.W. Silverwood	1	1	0	0	0	0.00	0

Catches: Stewart 19 (st. 2); Knight 11; Hussain 8; Crawley 7; Croft 4; Atherton, Cork 3; Thorpe 2; Caddick, Tufnell, Gough, Mullally, Silverwood 1

BOWLING	Overs	Mdns	Runs	Wkts	Best	Ave.
Silverwood	25	8	71	4	3–63	17.75
Croft	182.1	53	340	18	5–95	18.89
Gough	191.3	47	532	26	5–40	20.46
Caddick	87.5	25	174	8	4–45	21.75
Tufnell	214	66	434	14	4–61	31.00
White	41	9	118	3	2–51	39.33
Mullally	117	38	252	6	2–47	42.00
Cork	98.5	21	300	7	3–96	42.86

Also bowled: Thorpe 1–1–0–0

All First-Class Games

BATTING	M	Inns	N.O.	Runs	H.S.	Ave.	100s
A.J. Stewart	9	14	2	774	173	64.50	3
R.C. Russell	1	2	1	61	61*	61.00	0
J.P. Crawley	10	14	2	582	112	48.50	1
G.P. Thorpe	9	14	1	511	119	39.31	2
N. Hussain	10	16	0	583	139	36.44	2
D.G. Cork	5	6	2	128	59	32.00	0
N.V. Knight	10	17	1	508	114	31.75	1
M.A. Atherton	10	17	2	456	118	30.40	1
R.D.B Croft	8	10	1	196	80	21.78	0
R.C. Irani	2	4	1	59	40	19.67	0
A.R. Caddick	6	9	1	121	28	15.12	0
P.C.R. Tufnell	9	10	5	69	19*	13.80	0
C. White	5	6	1	69	22*	13.80	0
D. Gough	8	10	1	62	18	6.89	0
C.E.W. Silverwood	3	4	0	25	11	6.25	0
A.D. Mullally	5	6	0	32	21	5.33	0

Catches: Stewart 30 (st. 3); Knight 18; Crawley 11; Hussain 13; Atherton 10; Thorpe 8; Tufnell 6; Croft, Cork 4; Caddick, Gough, Russell, Silverwood 3; Mullally 2; Irani, White 1

BOWLING	Overs	Mdns	Runs	Wkts	Best	Ave.
Silverwood	88.2	23	242	15	6–44	16.13
Gough	276.3	63	802	44	6–64	18.22
White	90.4	18	273	14	4–15	19.50
Croft	305.3	82	652	28	5–95	23.28
Tufnell	356.3	110	785	29	5–58	27.06
Caddick	205.5	53	467	17	4–45	27.47
Mullally	164.4	52	370	13	4–52	28.46
Cork	147.5	34	441	14	3–18	31.50
Irani	22.1	4	67	2	2–13	33.50

Also bowled: Thorpe 5.4–2–12–1.